# The Role of the Academic Librarian

ANNE LANGLEY, EDWARD GRAY
AND K.T.L. VAUGHAN

**Chandos Publishing**

*Oxford · England · New Hampshire · USA*

Chandos Publishing (Oxford) Limited
Chandos House
5 & 6 Steadys Lane
Stanton Harcourt
Oxford OX29 5RL
UK
Tel: +44 (0) 1865 884447 Fax: +44 (0) 1865 884448
Email: info@chandospublishing.com
**www.library-chandospublishing.com**

Chandos Publishing USA
3 Front Street, Suite 331
PO Box 338
Rollinsford, NH 03869
USA
Tel: 603 749 9171 Fax: 603 749 6155
Email: BizBks@aol.com

First published in Great Britain in 2003

ISBN:
1 84334 057 7 (paperback)
1 84334 058 5 (hardback)

British Library Cataloguing-in-Publication Data.
A catalogue record for this book is available from the British Library.

The Publishers make no representation, express or implied, with regard to the accuracy of the information contained in this publication and cannot accept any legal responsibility or liability for any errors or omissions.

The material contained in this publication constitutes general guidelines only and does not represent to be advice on any particular matter. No reader or purchaser should act on the basis of material contained in this publication without first taking professional advice appropriate to their particular circumstances.

Typeset by Monolith – www.monolith.uk.com
Printed in the UK and USA

tan

# CHANDOS
## INFORMATION PROFESSIONAL SERIES

Chandos' new series of books are aimed at the busy information professional. They have been specially commissioned to provide the reader with an authoritative view of current thinking. They are designed to provide easy-to-read and (most importantly) practical coverage of topics that are of interest to librarians and other information professionals. If you would like a full listing of current and forthcoming titles, please visit our web site **www.library-chandospublishing.com** or contact Hannah Grace-Williams on email info@chandospublishing.com or telephone number +44 (0) 1865 884447.

**New authors:** we are always pleased to receive ideas for new titles; if you would like to write a book for Chandos, please contact Dr Glyn Jones on email gjones@chandospublishing.com or telephone number +44 (0) 1865 884447.

**Bulk orders:** some organisations buy a number of copies of our books. If you are interested in doing this, we would be pleased to discuss a discount. Please contact Hannah Grace-Williams on email info@chandospublishing.com or telephone number +44 (0) 1865 884447.

# Contents

# Acknowledgements

It is with deepest gratitude that all three authors thank our in-house copyeditor, Jennie Holton Fant. With her well-trained editing eye and her excitement about the field of academic librarianship, she brought the book to a higher level than we could have reached on our own. We'd also like to thank Dr Glyn Jones, our publisher at Chandos Publishing (Oxford) Ltd, for shepherding us through the process of writing this book with a minimum of pain. We appreciate the opportunity to write this book, and hope it will be the beginning of a long partnership among the authors, the editors, the publishers, and you, our readers.

# About the authors

**Anne Langley** has worked in academic libraries since 1987 and has been a professional librarian since 1993. Having been employed in four academic libraries and the library of a large national research laboratory, she holds the rank of Associate Librarian at Duke University. She has also held positions in almost all areas of an academic library: technical services, collections services, public services, administration, and on various digital projects. Her publications and presentations cover research and projects in all areas of academic librarianship. Organizational behaviour in libraries is the focus of her latest research and this book is just the beginning of the process.

**Edward Gray** is a science librarian at Duke University with ten years' experience of working in libraries. He received his BS in Geography from Louisiana State University and then went on to receive an MS in Geography and an MLIS from the University of Tennessee. He lives in Chapel Hill, North Carolina with his wife Pamela where he enjoys running marathons and reading histories.

**K.T.L. Vaughan** is a user services librarian at the University of North Carolina at Chapel Hill Health Sciences Library, currently specializing in information literacy instruction. She has also held positions in two other ARL institutions and a US Environmental Protection Agency library. She holds an AB in biology from Harvard University and an MSLS from UNC-CH. Her research interests include the information habits of scientists and clinicians, the librarian's role in bioinformatics research, and the recruitment, retention, and development of science librarians.

The authors can be contacted via the publishers.

# Introduction

Learning is not attained by chance, it must be sought for with ardor and attended to with diligence.

Abigail Adams

Why did we write this book? We felt that there was a strong need for it in the profession. Libraries are very slow to change. The question remains: how can we instigate change in such an atmosphere? We believe you start with individuals! Stepping up to our challenges on a personal level seemed the best way to get change started in our organizations. The people working in any given library are what make it unique. We believe that people who are prepared for change on a personal level are better able to cope with the constant change in the larger environment.

What are some of the major challenges facing academic librarians now? They include:

- changes in the production and dissemination of scholarly communication;
- changes in higher education;
- growth of technology inside and outside of the library:
  - new means of communicating with library patrons and colleagues;
  - materials in multiple formats, and read with varying systems, including mobile technologies;

– competition from the 'free web' and from commercial vendors and booksellers;

– technology in the workplace.

This book focuses mostly on improving the human resources in the library. Your specialized knowledge and your professional ethics are what make you, as a human resource, unique in your library. What do we need to change? We need to look outside the profession to other models of work behavior to see how we can do it better. What do we already do well? In library school and your initial training, you have learned the classic library functions of reference, collection management (including acquisitions and cataloging), access and information technology, and customer service. These are primarily organizational behaviors such as time management, networking, communication skills, leadership, etc. As professional librarians we know how to manage the library, but we don't instinctively know how to manage ourselves within the larger organization.

This type of change begins with you. It cannot be dictated from the top down. We are suggesting that you challenge yourself to learn how to work well within the larger organization. Hone your personal skills so that they don't get in the way of your library expertise. There is a real absence of leadership training in our profession – take it upon yourself to become a leader. We hope this book will get you started.

We begin the book with a chapter on *Time management*. In times of great change there is always a transition period, where you are simultaneously doing things the old *and* the new way. When you improve how you manage your time, you will be better prepared to accommodate change. Another bonus to improving your time management skills is that it makes you a better colleague and employee. When you can manage workdays with multiple meetings, get assignments in on time, and respond to queries immediately, you will be supporting everyone's efforts within the entire organization. It can be quite a drain on the work of the library to hold up an entire committee's work because you haven't done your part.

The next chapter, *Organizing*, covers a bit of quick theory on how technological advances in the workplace affect how we create and store information. We then quickly delve into ways to help you manage all the information you accumulate on all of your various projects, and in all of your multiple job duties. When you are better organized, it makes you a better colleague and employee. We want to ensure that you always have the information you need to do an excellent job right at your fingertips – and with the least amount of effort exerted to put it there.

The fourth chapter, *Communication*, is quite possibly the most important chapter in the book. If you can communicate well, you will be able to get more done, get others to support your ideas, and be a more efficient and effective colleague and employee. Poor communication skills get in the way of anything getting done. None of the work in the library is done in a vacuum. We have to work with others to get anything accomplished. So where do we learn communications skills? Hopefully this chapter will get you well on your way to improving your own skills.

The chapter on *Meetings* may possibly come as a surprise to some of you. Much of the work we do takes place in meetings. If you haven't accepted that yet, now is a good time to do so. Poorly run meetings are the main cause of why many of us don't think things can be accomplished in meetings. It is up to us to learn how to make these necessary activities work well.

With Chapter 6, *Collection development in the electronic world*, we switch gears a little to share with you some practical insights into how the increase in electronic materials has changed how we do what we do. This chapter also covers some of the new skills you will need to have in order to cope in this new environment. Chapter 7, *Public service in the electronic world*, does the same for public service activities. It gives you practical advice on the changes taking place and the skills you need to have to respond to these changes.

*Networking*, Chapter 8, covers how to get along in the politicized environment of the academic librarian. As much as we may want to push it under the rug, we work in very politicized environments. Where there are people, there will be politics. We describe some techniques to help the academic librarian weave their way through some of the major minefields.

The advice and tips in the chapter called *Moving up* will be of help to any academic librarian who takes the professional role of the librarian seriously. Sharing improvements in how we do our work in a change-is-constant environment is paramount to our profession's continued success.

The final chapter, *Leadership*, allows the reader to see a bigger view of their role in the academic library. We begin with an overview of the basics of supervision, and end the chapter with what we think are the basic tenets of leadership for academic librarians.

We hope that this book is just a beginning for you. At the end of every chapter is a reading list if you want to learn more. It is up to each of us as individuals to take charge of our own path of learning. Much of what we share with you in this book is timeless, though it may need a small amount of adaptation, as technology and other advances in knowledge alter the world around us. Some of the advice in this book may be out of date tomorrow. In any case, we hope that anything you take away from your reading of these words improves your professional life.

## Further reading

Vaill, Peter B. (1991) *Learning as a Way of Being*. San Francisco, CA: Jossey-Bass.

Wycoff, Joyce (1995) *Transformation Thinking*. New York: Berkeley Books.

# 2

# Time management

*I am long on ideas, but short on time. I only expect to live about a hundred years.*

Thomas Edison

The most successful professionals in any field are the ones who can finish multiple projects in an efficient and seemingly effortless manner. These people aren't blessed with some special power that sets them apart from the hoi polloi – they are just very good at managing their time. Unfortunately, time management skills are not taught in most professional library programs. Unless you developed good habits as a student or in a previous position, you may be feeling overwhelmed by the work filling your office. This is a common feeling, so don't feel guilty about all the work that's piling up. Instead, do something about it! This chapter will help you learn and apply the basic maxims of time management to your work habits, transforming you into an effective time manager.

## Maxims of time management

### *Everything takes time*

Those of us who ride buses on a regular basis are familiar with this principle. Think of it this way: your bus comes at

5:23. Your office is on the fifth floor in a building two blocks from the bus stop. What time do you need to leave for the bus? Well, everything takes time. First, you have to shut down your computer, gather your belongings, and put on your coat. Then you have to either catch the elevator or take the stairs. Then, walk the two blocks to the bus stop (which can take a varying amount of time depending on the weather and with whom you're walking). Then wait for the bus (which may or may not be on time!). Each individual action in this process takes time.

You probably schedule only the big events into your day. These may be meetings, classes, reference desk hours, office hours, or lunch. However, it is important to build into each activity some cushion time that accounts for all of the accompanying tasks, such as:

- *Travel time to an appointment.* Getting to a meeting or to a public service responsibility late can have serious consequences. Getting there early will not only make you feel relaxed, but can garner you a good reputation for punctuality and eagerness.

- *Production time for materials.* This includes time spent copying and assembling handouts, or waiting for a printer to process a large print job.

- *Computer issues.* These may be time spent booting up or shutting down your computer, opening and closing files, finding information on the computer, or synching your handheld device.

- *Trying to find lost or misplaced items.* As will be discussed later, a strong organizational scheme will save serious amounts of time. If you know where something is, you will spend less time looking for it!

## You are not an island

No matter where you are in the organizational hierarchy, there are other people who are willing and eager to help out on your projects. These may be other librarians, your staff, or student assistants. It seems like a lot of librarians are 'type A' personalities, who want to make sure that everything is done perfectly – and who worry that no one else will do things as well as they can. In reality, teamwork often produces better results than trying to accomplish everything individually.

When delegating steps in a project to other people, first determine what the steps are. Then, match steps to the skills and abilities of the people who can help. Give tasks requiring precision and accuracy, such as copyediting, to people with a keen eye for detail. Conversely, very creative people will enjoy doing more design-related aspects of a project. If you are nervous about sharing your projects, you might want to work on the critical steps yourself – that way you retain ownership and control over the core of the project while getting help on other areas.

It is easier to delegate when you know and acknowledge your own strengths and weaknesses. For example, if you are good at starting projects but not at finishing them, delegate the first draft to an idea person. Just because it is your project doesn't mean you have to have your finger in every part of it. Do what you do best, and delegate to others to share their strength and expertise.

You will find that one of the most important time management or personal management skills is the art of delegation. Librarians who are able to share projects in an effective and efficient manner generally acquire images as 'team players' and good managers. Librarians who do not lead teams to accomplish tasks will be seen as 'loners.' In today's world, team players get promoted – loners get fired.

## *Do the critical stuff first*

A friend once opined that there are two types of people: those who write 'to-do' lists and those who don't. To-do lists are excellent tools for brainstorming tasks ahead, but they have two major flaws. First, putting everything possible on the list may depress you and cause you to get even *less* done than you might have accomplished otherwise. Secondly, but more importantly, few people prioritize their lists. Most of us have a tendency to work on our lists in an organic, unstructured way – doing the tasks and projects first that are easiest or that we enjoy the most. This tactic works some of the time, but when a large, critical project that you are not looking forward to comes along, you may discover you are pressed for time because of having done the fun stuff first.

The moral here: prioritize your daily, weekly, and monthly tasks. Reevaluate your priorities on a regular basis. Do the projects that absolutely must get done first. One effective means of prioritizing your projects is to plan out your work time over the course of a week. Set aside designated times for the critical projects in each day. Make sure you don't let small jobs such as answering e-mail encroach on 'project time.' It is particularly important for known procrastinators – you know who you are – to force yourselves to prioritize.

## *Librarian, know thyself*

Take a moment to think about your work habits in relation to your daily rhythms. Are you a morning or evening person? You probably have times of the day during which you are very sharp and alert. These are the times when you should be working on the most demanding projects, the ones that require the most concentration. At other times, you may be tired and not as quick. Reserve the daily chores that require less brainpower for these times. By matching your daily tasks to your 'alertness cycle' you will be able to accomplish the most important tasks in a more consistently efficient manner.

Another self-examination that you should periodically assess is your personal and environmental health. If you feel stressed and overworked, your health will suffer. On the other hand, if you feel tired or ill, you will likely become stressed at work. Some questions to ask yourself are:

- Am I sleeping enough?
- Am I eating correctly and drinking enough water?
- Am I getting enough exercise?
- Do I have a life outside work?

A 'no' answer to any of these questions should alert you to issues that could be affecting your work efficiency. It is important to take care of yourself, and not just so that you can be your best at work!

## A place for everything, and everything in its place

As mentioned earlier in this chapter, one of the most insidious time-wasters is searching for lost items. This can be anything from a misplaced sock to that report you were supposed to read and which is somewhere in the black hole of your office. Having a good organizational scheme, whether it is a filing system, a 'piling' system, or a great secretary, will help you save time *and* look good to visiting faculty and supervisors.

Organization is dealt with in-depth elsewhere in this book. However, one note: as with everything else, keeping your office area organized *takes time*. This is a great task to do during one of your 'down times', such as first thing in the morning or right before lunch. One author of this book considers Fridays after 3 p.m. her 'cleanup time.' Coworkers are skipping out early for the weekend (physically or mentally), so there is usually no one around. Friday afternoon does not seem a reasonable time to start a new project but this is still productive time for her, so she spends it organizing and planning for the next week.

## Practice makes perfect

As with every other skill, being a good time manager takes time and continuous effort. It is all well and good to purchase a calendar or to do a time audit (see time management tools no. 1 and no. 2 later in this chapter), but if you do not bother to keep up with them, they will be useless. Those of us who are naturally disorganized or procrastinators must continually work on our skills.

## 'All work and no play makes Jack a dull boy' (with apologies to Stephen King, The Shining)

Okay, so it's unlikely that if you spend all day working at the library you will lose it and take an axe to your spouse and child. But burnout does happen in our profession, and one of the first symptoms is the feeling that you don't have enough time in the day to complete all of your work. However, it *is* likely that you aren't using the time you have in an efficient manner, probably because you've neglected one of the maxims above.

Remember that you are not just your job – you are also a person. As a human being, you have certain needs, including the need for food, rest, exercise, and human companionship. First, you need a break. Get up from your desk. Get out of your office. Go outside if the weather is nice, or to a lounge or other non-stressful place. Go out for a quick lunch with friends and/or coworkers. Bring your knitting or a book to work, and take ten minutes to relax. Many workplaces are starting yoga programs to encourage healthy activity at work. Even a quick walk can refresh your mind and spirit, leaving you energized and ready to face whatever that next task may be.

While it may have been true ten years ago, it is no longer impressive to tell everyone how busy you are. They will take it to mean that you have poor time management skills. It is up to you to manage your time so that things get done and you don't get burned out doing them.

# The calendar: time management tool no. 1

> If you want to make an apple pie from scratch, you must first create the universe.
>
> Carl Sagan

No librarian should be without some kind of calendar. Whether it is a simple notebook or a fancy Franklin-Covey DayPlanner, a pen-and-paper system or an online corporate calendaring software system, the calendar is an absolutely essential tool for time management and scheduling.

Why is the calendar so important? The most common use of the calendar is to prompt you to go to meetings or finish certain projects. As a memory aid, it is indispensable – nothing will wreck your career faster than forgetting to show up for an important meeting or for your scheduled shift at a public service point. Take into consideration the effect your lateness has on your colleagues' impression of you. They will have to pick up the slack. Second, calendars are vital for effective scheduling. Your personal calendar helps keep you from double-booking meetings. A group calendar facilitates the scheduling of meetings, public service duties, laboratory or shared computer time, and so on. Finally, a public calendar (particularly one that is online) can help people find you in an emergency.

Selecting a calendar that works for you can be a complicated process. You need to take your needs and habits into account, including such factors as:

- Do you schedule most of your work while at your computer or while outside of your office?

- Do you like to make notes about what each meeting will entail, tasks to accomplish, and/or outcomes?
- Do you need something portable because you spend most of your time on the move?
- Do you feel more comfortable using low-tech or high-tech systems?
- Do you need to share your calendar with other groups?

The answers to these questions will help you determine what calendar is best for you. The most popular options currently include print date books with pages for one day, a week, or a month at a time; personal digital assistants (PDAs) on which you can both keep a calendar and a notepad; and online networked group calendars. Successful professionals use one or more of these tools.

Above all else, remember that having a calendar and using a calendar are different things! In order for your calendar to be helpful you *must* keep it up to date. Otherwise it is little more than a waste of money.

# Tips for managing the major time drains

## *E-mail*

E-mail can be an awesome time saver. Because of e-mail you may not have to sit through dull meetings. You can share files, have quick discussions, and keep up with distant colleagues. On the other hand, you could be getting so much e-mail in the course of one day that you can't imagine reading it all, much less responding. The proliferation of junk e-mail (aka spam), chain letters, duplicative postings to listservs, and other uninteresting e-mail can clutter your inbox and make it difficult to find the important messages.

Make it easier on yourself, and follow these simple tips for controlling your e-mail:

- Don't subscribe to every listserv imaginable. Just one or two will suffice.
- Keep your e-mail address off webpages, or list it using one of the 'anti-spam' e-mail address formats (e.g. my_name [at] school [dot] edu). Many direct-e-mail lists are generated using addresses pulled off the Internet.
- Make folders in your e-mail system and have messages forwarded directly into them.
- Set aside a limited amount of time to respond to e-mail every day. Respond to critical messages immediately, but leave the rest for later.

The chapters on organization and communication have more information about using e-mail.

## The Web

You may have the best of intentions when you open up your web browser. 'I'm just checking the weather.' 'I want to see what the hours are for that branch library.' 'I'm looking up something for a patron.' But how often does the good intention derail when you see an interesting ad, or remember something that you meant to buy or look up for your personal use? Surfing the Web can be a very relaxing activity for a break, but be careful that you don't let it become a time-draining habit.

To keep the Web at bay:

- close the browser window when you've found the piece of information you need;

- if you are browsing the Web on a break, mark a time when you will go back to work. If you know you are bad at keeping a deadline, bring in an egg timer and set it to go off after 10 or 15 minutes.

## Meetings

Meetings can drain your time in two ways. First, the meeting that runs shorter than or exactly within its allotted time is rare to the point of extinction. Most meetings, in our experience, are prolonged. Second, librarians have a tendency to meet to discuss even the most minute issues. This leads to a proliferation of meetings that do not produce results.

Clearly, the meeting facilitator's skills with meetings will affect how time is spent. However, as a participant you can help keep a meeting on track. Here are some tips:

- Keep your off-target comments to yourself, or write them down to be shared later.

- If the meeting is veering off course, interject a summarizing statement or observation. This will usually bring discussion to a close and will garner you a reputation as an astute observer and participant.

- Prepare your report or other materials in advance of the meeting and distribute copies to participants *before* you get there. Then you can spend time in the meeting going over the main points of the document without wasting time going over every detail.

- Read supplementary materials before the meeting. Be prepared to comment on them.

- Bring your calendar to every meeting. This way, if there is a conflict, a subsequent meeting can be scheduled without delay.

As a new librarian a proliferation of meetings is often out of your hands. You may be assigned to groups, and you may be pressured to 'volunteer' for others. However, there are some simple ways to cut back on the number of meetings you attend:

- Evaluate the groups to which you belong. Are any irrelevant to your work or career?

- If you feel that you are spending too much time in meetings, talk to your supervisor. He or she will probably understand, sympathize, and work with you to resolve the problem.

- Some of the work of committees can realistically be done electronically. Suggest utilizing electronic meetings or e-mail discussions in place of physical ones, as appropriate.

Chapter 5 on meetings covers these and other issues in much more depth.

## Long-term projects

When a long-term project is first assigned, you may feel that you have plenty of time to finish it. However, a few weeks or months later when the deadline looms, you may wonder where all that time went. Managing a long-term project well requires following all of the time management maxims, not least of which would be delegating and prioritizing steps. The easiest way to complete projects with a minimum of stress is to use the following tips:

- Break the project up into small steps or chunks, each with its own deadline. This way you have multiple little things to do over shorter periods of time rather than one monster project due way down the road.

- Prioritize the most important steps to complete first. Figure out which critical steps depend on other steps. Determine which steps can be done concurrently.

- Delegate tasks to colleagues, staff, and students who are interested in the project. Make sure everyone knows their tasks *and* their deadlines.

- Give yourself plenty of time at the end to assemble all of the disparate parts into a seamless whole.

## The time audit: time management tool no. 2

Think you've got a problem with time management? One excellent way to diagnose where your time goes is to do a time audit (sometimes called a 'time use study'). Just like a financial audit, this exercise forces you to examine where you are spending your time. The time audit is sometimes done by an entire library or department with the aid of a business consultant, but can also be scaled down to the level of a single professional.

Like everything else, the time audit takes time. However, it is fairly simple to set up, run, and analyze. The data collected will be the amount of time you spend on any given task, including seemingly brief ones such as breaks, e-mail, and walking to appointments.

## Steps in the time audit

1. Create daily worksheets with cells or other spaces for each hour in the day. Produce enough worksheets for each day of the period being studied (usually a week or a month). The worksheet is often printed out to facilitate ease of use, but could also be computerized using Microsoft Excel or an online calendaring tool.

2. To begin a day, mark on the sheet the time you arrived at work. From this point until you leave, write down every time you end a task or activity (even breaks!) and start a new one, with a note about what it is you are doing.

3. Try not to act differently from how you usually do. It can be tempting to 'be good' so that you look better on paper, but this only sabotages your results.

4. At the end of the day, note the time you leave work.

5. Repeat this process for the duration of the study period.

6. After the study is over, code your activities according to major job function. If you are a reference librarian, you might have categories for time spent at the reference desk, teaching classes, answering e-mail, in library meetings, in non-library meetings, doing professional and continuing

education activities, traveling, taking breaks, and working on major projects.

7. Sum up over the course of each day and the total time period the amount and percent of time spent in each activity.

8. Given your job functions, what areas seem suspiciously over- or under-committed? You may be surprised at the amount of time you spend walking to meetings, answering e-mail, or doing other marginal activities.

9. Brainstorm in what ways you can alter your work habits and priorities to emphasize in terms of time the important aspects of your professional life.

## Conclusion

This chapter comes at the very beginning of the book for a reason – time is your most precious commodity. The better able you are to manage your time, the better job you will be able to do. Take care of what is easy first, the stuff you actually have control over, like your time, and then when the hard stuff comes along, you will be prepared to face it. Get your time and especially your calendar under control, and you will feel more like you too are in control.

## Further reading

Cochran, J. Wesley (1992) *Time Management Handbook for Librarians*. New York: Greenwood Press.

Davidson, Jeff (1995) *The Complete Idiot's Guide to Managing Your Time*. New York: Alpha Books.

DeFord, Vicki (1997) 'Time management,' *The Unabashed Librarian*, 104: 14–16.

Hayes, Sherman (1993) 'Accounting for your time!', *The Bottom Line*, 7: 32–7.

Line, Maurice B. (2001) 'Busyness and profitable activity: how should managers spend their time. Part 1,' *Library Management*, 22, 8/9: 416.

Line, Maurice B. (2002) 'How should managers spend their time? Part 2,' *Library Management*, 23, 1/2: 101–2.

Masterton, Alisa (1997) *Getting Results with Time Management*. London: Library Association Publishing.

Mayer, Jeffrey J. (1999) *Time Management for Dummies*. Foster City, CA: IDG Books Worldwide.

Morgenstern, Julie (2000) *Time Management from the Inside Out: The Foolproof System for Taking Control of Your Schedule and Your Life*. New York: Henry Holt.

Nofsinger, Mary M. (1996) 'Time management skills: a checklist,' *College and Research Libraries News*, 10: 648–50.

Nofsinger, Mary (1997) 'Managing work time,' in Joan Giesecke (ed.), *Practical Help for New Supervisors*. Chicago: American Library Association.

Pandora, Cherie Pettit (1992) 'Time management for the overworked, understaffed, library/media specialist,' *Ohio Media Spectrum*, 44: 67–70.

Peterson, Lisa C. (1997) 'Time management for library professionals,' *Katharine Sharp Review*, 5, Summer; online at *http://alexia.lis.uiuc.edu/review/5/peterson.html*.

Siess, Judith A. (2002) *Time Management, Planning, and Prioritization for Librarians.* Lanham, MD: Scarecrow Press.

'Time in the bank: a special collection of time-saving tips that will put you in control of your schedule,' *Library Personnel News*, 13, 3/4 (2000): 13.

Walster, Dian (1993) *Managing Time: A How-To-Do-It Manual for Librarians*, How-To-Do-It Manuals for School and Public Librarians, No. 12. New York: Neal-Schuman Publishers.

Watkins, Denise M. (1999) 'Are you a time management junkie?' *Information Outlook*, 3, 1: 34–5.

# 3

# Organizing

*Is not the whole world a vast house of assignation of which the filing system has been lost?*

Quentin Crisp

Most companies frown upon the stacks of memos, reports, articles, and books that create clutter in their employees' offices. In a recent *Economist* article, it was reported that several companies, including United Parcel Service and General Motors, have 'clean desk' policies – all evidence of work must be removed from desks by the end of each working day. One company, the advertising firm Chiat/Day, tried getting rid of desks and filing cabinets altogether so there would be no places to keep paper. In the age of information technology and networked workplaces, paper and its resultant clutter is considered old-fashioned and inefficient by office managers.

One would think that with our professional specialty in information technology and skills in organizing and classifying, librarians would not appear to be likely candidates for having clutter in their offices. Such is not the case. A first boss and mentor of an author of this book had just retired after having worked in the same library since 1965. As she packed away all her numerous piles of paper, a startling discovery was made – her piles of paperwork were covering an actual desk that had not seen the light of day since 1966.

Should you step into the office of this author's current boss, you would see mountains of papers, articles and books with paperclips, rubber bands, and pens located in the valleys below. Rumor has it that this boss, too, has a desk hidden underneath those piles, which she hurriedly makes apparent when her own boss visits. On the other hand, another author of this book can clearly see the desk in his office. Occasionally, his desk becomes cluttered with piles amid empty used diet soda cans, but this state of affairs makes him jittery. Before too much desk surface disappears, he either files items away, or recycles them. Knowing that items in his office are in their proper place brings peace of mind.

So here comes the part where you'd expect us to say that the author is better organized than his former and current supervisors. With his desk usually so neat and tidy, you'd think he would boast that he is more efficient than colleagues whose desks look like they have been hit by a twister. Most books on organizing would say that he is more efficient, because all his papers and files have a 'proper' place and non-essential items are nicely filed away, creating a clutter-free environment. So he's better organized, right? Well, not necessarily. A seemingly messy office can be as well organized as an office in which no scrap of paper is out of place. Although the opinions of managers and business consultants may differ, you'd be hard-pressed to find a strong correlation between clutter and inefficiency. Piles of papers may give you quicker access to information than do nicely labeled files that have been hidden away in cabinets. Piles can offer you visual clues of your work in progress, including what tasks are pressing and need attention.

So if clutter isn't necessarily a bad thing, should you even bother with having a system of organizing your desk and office? Of course! Even librarians with seemingly random piles of papers on their desks have a general organizing principle for their office. One librarian we know gets hassled by management because every surface in his office has at least four feet of books and papers on it. However, he can find any item in his office faster than most librarians with clean desks and well-labeled files. He's efficient because he has a system, and uses it consistently.

But wait – won't clutter become a moot point as more information is transmitted digitally and paper disappears? Actually, it is quite the reverse. The first part of this chapter looks at why the amount of information you receive at work, in both print and electronic formats will only continue to increase in the future. Next we move on to strategies for organizing your paper, as well as your e-mail and computer files. Because no one system of organizing works for everyone, feel free to pick and choose the tips that work best for you. Once you find a strategy that's helpful, stick with it.

## The information explosion

With the rise of personal computers and networking in offices during the 1970s and 1980s, business journalists and trend watchers predicted the time of the paperless office was coming in the near future. Look around your desk and your colleagues' desks and see if that is the case. In *The Myth of the Paperless Office*, Abigail Sellen and Richard Harper posit two trends that seem to ensure paper's continued viability. The first trend is that increases in network bandwidth have made more information available to people at work and home than ever before. Once received, this information is easily sent on to others who are also connected. Many people can only make sense of all this incoming information if it is printed. Sellen and Harper cite a study that found there is a 40 percent increase in paper consumption in organizations that introduce e-mail to their workers. The second trend is that new print technologies make it easy to produce low-cost, high-quality printed documents. True, many documents are being created digitally and sent over networks, which does not require the need for paper. However, once again people are printing these documents instead of reading them on a computer screen. This is born out by the fact that sales of printers increased by 600 percent from 1988 to 1993.

Most of us are also experiencing what the Lotus Development researchers Steve Whittaker and Candace Sidner call 'e-mail overload.' Originally, e-mail was created as an application for asynchronous communication. Soon people were using it for task management and personal archiving, functions for which it was not designed. With e-mail now being used to deliver documents, delegate work, track tasks, schedule appointments, send reminders, store contact information, and ask for assistance, it's no surprise that our inboxes are so full.

# Managing your paper files

When most of you got your first professional job in a library, you probably had little idea that you would have to devise a filing system. Graduate studies didn't require much filing – you just had to keep all your notes and assignments from a given class in a three-ring binder or a folder. At home, you may have some basic files for items like taxes and bills. Unfortunately, such rudimentary systems don't prepare you for the onslaught of paper you'll see at work.

Research has shed some light on how we work with paper. Whittaker and Hirschberg studied how office workers judge, manage, and store paper documents. Their research shows that for every document received, we must make the following three judgements:

1. the value of the document;
2. whether and how to categorize the document;
3. whether to keep the document available for immediate use or file it away for later.

The tips below will get you started on the road to managing your files effectively. Remember, everyone has a different system of organizing their paper documents. Be willing to experiment, but stick with a system if it gives you good results.

■ *Trash your junk immediately.* While the value of a document isn't always apparent as soon as you receive it, some items are obviously meant for the trash can. It's easy to put these worthless documents to one side and forget about them. Instead, go ahead and get rid of them as soon as you receive them. Don't let them obscure more important documents.

- *Don't wait to deal with the easy items.* Sometimes you get documents that can be acted on right away. These papers might just need a signature or a simple response before they can be sent on. Deal with these documents as soon as you get them.

- *Date your documents.* Writing the date in the corner of your documents can help you place them in context. This is especially useful when you're flipping through a pile of papers related to a particular project. The dates help you make sense of the project's workflow by seeing the temporal relationships between the documents.

  Dating documents also lets you know if you need to take any action. Let's suppose a patron requests an item. Make a copy of the request and date it. If the patron complains because he or she hasn't received the item, you can easily see when the request was made. This lets you know if you should wait (too little time has elapsed), or if you should act (too much time has elapsed).

- *Keep working documents together.* Pretty obvious advice, no? Keep all documents related to a particular project or committee together and have them near at hand. Consider placing them in a folder so they don't get mixed up with other papers. You can easily flip through them to see the progress of your work, or take them to a meeting, if they are grouped together. Working documents shouldn't be archived until a project is complete.

- *Don't file prematurely.* Whittaker and Hirschberg studied the paper processing activities of two different groups: filers, who tend to have clean desks, and pilers, who have offices dominated by clutter. Contrary to their expectations, filers generally had larger archives and kept documents of lower value than pilers. Filers often adopt complex and time-consuming filing schemes that give them little time to decide the worth of documents. Pilers, on the other hand, have greater accessibility to recent information and do a better job of cleaning up their archives. The only danger for pilers is that their information becomes inaccessible once piles start to multiply. Try becoming a piler in moderation. Not filing papers right away gives you time to decide if they are worthwhile to you.

- *Discard!* Don't attach sentimental value to every piece of paper that crosses your desk. Whittaker and Hirschberg found that only 49 percent of the documents in paper files were unique. When you consider filing an item, ask yourself whether you have a foreseeable need for it and whether you could access the item somewhere else. If the answers are no and yes, respectively, go ahead and throw that item away.

- *Move it if you're not using it.* Keep documents away from the center of your desktop or workspace if you don't have an immediate need for them. This doesn't mean they have to be filed away. Put them in a pile to the side to file later, when you have decided where they belong.

- *Be flexible with file names.* Once you do decide to put away a document into a filing cabinet, you have to come up with some headings for the file folders. You might find this to be a difficult task if you are uncertain of your job priorities or emphasis. Be willing to alter your filing scheme until you get a good sense of what type of documents you want to archive.

## Managing your e-mail

At first glance, managing your e-mail appears analogous to managing your paper files. Just like with paper documents, you have to decide with each e-mail: (i) what its value is to you; (ii) whether you should categorize it; and (iii) whether you should file it. Your e-mail inbox is similar to your desktop. Keep the documents you are currently working on in your inbox just as you do with paper documents on your desk. Folders in your e-mail system can be used just like folders in a filing cabinet. However, there are differences between the two. Managing your e-mail is physically easier than managing your paper files. All you have to do is press a button to send, file, or delete your e-mail messages. With most e-mail systems, you can access your e-mail messages from any connected computer, unless the server is down.

Here are some tips for managing your e-mail files. Some are similar to the tips for working with paper files; some are unique for e-mail. Organizing e-mail requires a delicate balance between knowing what to keep, and what to delete.

■ *Write or copy it down.* Many of your e-mail messages contain information about incoming appointments. Copy dates and other important information into your planner or calendar and then delete or file the message.

- *Delete useless messages.* Don't bother to keep messages you aren't going to read or use. All you have to do is click a button to delete them.

- *Use folders.* Without folders, you will constantly be scrolling through your inbox to find pertinent messages. Transfer useful, but not immediately necessary, messages into folders. In most e-mail systems, it's easy to create folders and even nest folders within other folders.

- *Don't file prematurely.* You don't want to file your e-mails too soon. Often, e-mails remind you of work that is in progress and what actions you need to perform. Moving e-mails from your inbox to a folder might cause you to forget about, and thereby lose track of, your workflow. Keep pertinent messages in your inbox or in folders you are certain to visit.

- *Watch out for 'failed folders'.* According to Whittaker and Sidner, 'failed folders' are folders that you create, but that don't reduce the complexity of your e-mail management. This can be because your folders are too small and contain only one or two items, or because they are too big and unwieldy. If you regularly file your messages into folders, you are less likely to have 'failed folders.'

- *Archive your e-mail.* The nice thing about e-mail is that it doesn't pile up and clutter your office like paper documents. However, some systems limit the amount of disk space allotted for your e-mail messages. To keep space free, regularly archive older messages onto a local hard disk.

# Managing your computer files

The number of computer files you create, whether they are word processing, spreadsheet, presentation, or other documents, will no doubt be significantly fewer than the number of paper and e-mail messages you receive. However, your non-e-mail computer files can become unmanageable and cause you to waste time locating needed documents. Here are a few tips to help you with organizing your computer files:

- *Place your documents in folders.* Just like paper documents and e-mail messages, you can easily place your computer files into folders. Group them by types of work you are doing, or by the names of the committees and tasks forces you are working on.

- *Think about your file names.* It's hard to remember the names of files several months after you create them. Try choosing names that are distinct and descriptive. Also, think about how you name files that go through frequent rounds of editing. Adding terms like 'new,' 'newer,' and 'final new' create confusion. Naming conventions are a hot topic for departments and teams that share files. It's a good idea to standardize file-naming rules so everyone can find what they need.

- *Sort by date.* Computer files can be sorted in different ways such as alphabetically, by date, or by size. If you set up your file manager to sort by date, the files you are working on will come up first.

# Conclusion

Building on the time management skills you learned in the first chapter and after reading this chapter on organizing we hope you will now have many more hours in your workday to tackle the skills discussed in the next chapter on communication. You now have the basics of your own office under control, now it is time to broaden your reach.

# Further reading

Dale, Denise (2000) 'Getting and staying organized: focus on personal papers,' *Feliciter*, 46, 1: 38–40.

Gleeson, Kerry (1998) *The High-Tech Personal Efficiency Program: Organizing Your Electronic Resources to Maximize Your Time and Efficiency*. New York: John Wiley & Sons.

'In praise of clutter' (2002) *The Economist*, 21 December, pp. 86–8.

McCormack, Mark H. (2000) *Getting Results for Dummies*. Foster City, CA: IDG Books Worldwide.

Morgenstern, Julie (1998) *Organizing from the Inside Out: The Foolproof System for Organizing Your Home, Your Office, and Your Life*. New York: Henry Holt.

Roth, Eileen and Miles, Elizabeth (2001) *Organizing for Dummies*. Foster City, CA: IDG Books Worldwide.

Sellen, Abigail J. and Harper, Richard H.R. (2002) *The Myth of the Paperless Office*. Cambridge, MA: MIT Press.

Whittaker, Steve and Hirschberg, Julia (2001) 'The character, value and management of personal paper archives,' *ACM Transactions on Computer Human Interaction*, 8: 150–70.

Whittaker, Steve and Sidner, Candace (1996) 'Email overload: exploring personal information management of email,' available online at: *http://doi.acm.org/10.1145/238386.238530*.

# 4

# Communication

The man who goes alone can start today; but he who travels with another must wait till the other is ready.

Henry David Thoreau

Here's a challenge: try to find a job ad from the last five years for an academic library position that doesn't ask for 'excellent communication skills' as a qualification. After skimming numerous ads, you will notice that required and preferred qualifications can vary widely, but almost all ads stress the need for communication skills, both verbal and written. Next to having a recognized professional qualification, being a good communicator is the primary job skill that employers look for.

What exactly is meant by good or excellent communication skills? Do you have to be a wonderful orator, able to hold your audiences spellbound with your every word? Do you have to be an unsurpassed wordsmith, with every e-mail message worthy of a Pulitzer? Not quite. It means that you are able to convey your thoughts, ideas, and work to others in a manner that is clear and succinct. Clarity and brevity matter. This is true regardless of the size of your audience and communication channel, whether you are e-mailing a single patron, writing a memo to faculty, or giving a presentation at a large library conference.

Communication is not just a one-way street. Although it's important that you successfully convey information in your work environment, it's equally important that you receive and understand information from your patrons and colleagues. Active listening and thoughtful reading will help you go far in your career. It pays to heed the advice of colleagues, especially in matters of dealing with patrons or handling office politics.

This chapter focuses on communication in two realms. The first is communication in your day-to-day work. Increasingly, you will find much of this dominated by e-mail correspondence, especially if you work at a larger library with many departments and branches. However, you should not let e-mail get in the way of telephone and face-to-face conversations when appropriate, as they can often be more meaningful than electronic communications. The second realm is communication in the larger, professional environment. Although you may have had enough of learning theories and models of practice in library school, you should still keep current with cutting-edge librarianship. Doctors and lawyers are required to keep up with the state of the art in their fields; librarians must do the same.

## Communicating at work

A major misconception most people have about librarians is that they get to read all day at work. The reality is that on many days at work you will never even touch a book, because you're too busy interacting with others. These people may be patrons, coworkers, or vendors, but it's always *somebody*.

Librarians are in the people business. You will quickly realize that most of your day is taken up by responding to e-mail, fielding phone calls, and attending meetings. In this section, we will review the most common forms of communication and how they can be made more profitable.

## E-mail

In 1988, one of the co-authors got his first library job as a student assistant at a large university library. While working in the main office, he was amazed that the assistant director sent and received messages from a computer via phone lines. Out of a staff of 150, the assistant director was the only employee who corresponded electronically. How things have changed in 15 years! Employers now consider knowing how to use e-mail a basic competency. Unfamiliarity with e-mail is almost akin to being unable to tie your shoe laces. It's all right if you don't want to communicate by e-mail – just don't plan on working.

E-mail has become the most prominent means of communication in many library settings. This is especially true for larger libraries that are spread over many departments and branches. It is easier and faster to communicate with numerous coworkers by e-mail than by sending paper memos. Many librarians also communicate with patrons via e-mail. This will only increase as more library resources are made available online, and as patrons access these resources from their offices or homes. Instead of coming to the library with their reference needs, patrons are increasingly finding it simpler to e-mail their requests or questions.

The best feature of e-mail is that it is asynchronous communication. This means that the receivers of an e-mail message don't have to be logged into their computers when the message is sent. You can ask or answer questions any hour of the day. However, the worst feature of e-mail is also that it is asynchronous communication. Often you want a response right away when you communicate electronically. Since the receiver doesn't have to be around to get the message, you don't know when you will get a response. It can be a couple of minutes, a day, a week, or even longer before you hear back from the person you e-mailed. You may never get a response. Other forms of communication may be more appropriate if you need an immediate response. In those cases, the phone, or actually visiting someone's office, may be a better means of getting the speedy response you need.

Here are some tips to use e-mail more effectively:

- *Get to the point.* Most of us are bombarded with information at work. This will only get worse as more and more information is transmitted digitally. Most people only scan what comes across their computer screens. Given that fact, it's imperative to get to the point in your e-mails. Make sure your subject headings reflect the content of your e-mail. Don't wait until the final paragraph of your message to make your point. Consider using bullets and keeping your content to one screen or less, to make your message stand out.

- *Think about your tone.* People can't see you when you write an e-mail. They can't pick up winks, a rolling of the eyes, or changes in your voice. Most people will take what you write in your e-mails literally. Consequently, it is not wise to attempt sarcasm, irony, or wit in your messages. Unless you are e-mailing close acquaintances, who know your personality well, assume people are going to read what you write, not what you mean.

- *Check your spelling, grammar, and facts.* E-mails are not as formal as typed correspondence. They are not expected to win any prizes for grammar. However, multiple grammar mistakes and misspellings make it difficult for the reader to get through your messages. Read over your message before you send it. Often, you will catch numerous typos on a single read through. Most e-mail programs have a spellcheck that will only take a short time to run – use it! Make sure you've listed the correct time, place, and date of any appointments. A typo can be disastrous!

- *Share the wealth.* Don't be too restrictive about who you send your e-mails to. Your goals are often better served when you send information to more recipients, not fewer. *Never* depend on someone else to share your e-mail. If multiple people need to know something, send it to all of them. This allows everyone to be on board with the latest decisions or issues.

- *Read your mail carefully.* It's easy to miss a meeting because you didn't read an e-mail properly. *10:30* might look like *11:30* if you scan your e-mail too quickly. If there is important information in a message, make sure you copy it into a date book or calendar program, onto your to-do list, or save the message to a folder where you can get to it easily.

- *Respond promptly.* Occasionally you will send out an e-mail but never get a response. When it happens to you, it initially brings out your insecurities. Eventually you may become annoyed and start to view the other person in a negative light. Responding to e-mails is not hard to do. Even if you don't have time to send a proper response, at least acknowledge that you got the e-mail and will respond later.

- *Consider a second account.* Are you getting too many e-mails from friends at your work address? Look into getting a second account for personal business. Never give out your primary work address to businesses when you fill out an online form or survey. Many businesses sell addresses to third-party companies who create 'direct marketing' (i.e. spam or junk mail) e-mail lists.

## Face-to-face meetings

As much as librarians use e-mail, sometimes you just have to get away from your computer to communicate with others. You might have a team project which is easier to work on in person than by e-mail. You may need to show a patron how to use a database in his office or on his computer. Occasionally you will need to communicate highly personal information, for which e-mail is not appropriate. Some people just don't use e-mail, but you will still need to communicate with them. We hope this will not be you!

Consider the following when you have face-to-face meetings with others:

- *Come with questions or an agenda.* It is very frustrating to go to a meeting where the discussion is scattered all over the place, or nobody has anything to contribute. Take time before any meeting and consider the points you want to address. If you are running the meeting, come up with an agenda and share it with the participants in advance.

- *Limit the chitchat.* It is fun to socialize with coworkers or patrons, but too much will get in the way of your work. It's all right to spend a few minutes of any meeting catching up and shooting the bull, but don't forget the task at hand. When 15 to 30 minutes of a meeting are taken up with idle chatter, the meeting will probably be disorganized and run late.

- *Listen carefully to others.* It's easy to go to a meeting and forget by the next day what was covered and what was expected of you. Prevent this by listening carefully, and taking notes whenever possible. Active listening is especially critical when dealing with patrons. Often the stated request is not actually what the person wants. By staying carefully attuned, you can make the reference interview more useful for your patrons.

Chapter 5 on meetings has more details on these and other issues.

## Telephone calls

When you need information right away and e-mail and face-to-face meetings might not do the trick fast enough, the most efficient way to contact others may be by telephone.

Your patrons may feel the same way and prefer to reach you by telephone. This is especially true if you are working on a reference desk and/or manning the reference telephone line.

Think about the following when you communicate by telephone:

- *Clearly identify yourself.* Don't be a nameless representative of your library. Let others know who you are when they call so they have a future point of contact. Service-oriented librarians develop this skill quickly.

- *Write it down.* Take notes when you are on the phone or immediately after you hang up, so that you don't forget the conversation, or fail to pass along a message to a coworker.

- *Make it brief.* It is fine to chitchat for hours on the phone with your friends, but it's not wise to do the same in a professional setting. People have busy lives – let them get off the phone quickly.

## Keeping current

Librarianship has transformed itself rapidly with advances in information technology. You can't assume that the profession will remain static. Doctors, lawyers, and engineers keep up with new developments in their areas; librarians ought to do the same. Unless you want to jeopardize the advancement of your career, it's important to keep current with the state of our profession.

Fortunately, the information technology that is so rapidly changing our profession also makes it easy for you to stay current with librarianship. Without leaving your computer, you can find out the latest bibliographic instruction techniques, read reviews of databases and electronic products, and learn about censorship issues, all by using discussion lists, online journals, and websites. You can also stay current by browsing your periodicals section and attending professional meetings and talks.

## Discussion lists

A discussion list is a listing of e-mail names and addresses that are grouped under a single name. When an e-mail message is sent to the list, everyone in the group gets a copy of the message. This allows a message to be disseminated to a large group without having to send the message to multiple e-mail addresses. The most well-known type of discussion list in the US is the LISTSERV®, which was created by the LSoft company and is used by many academic and corporate institutions.

There are thousands of discussion lists devoted to a wide range of topics. Many deal specifically with issues in library science. These library lists are good places to learn about new technologies and resources, useful reference and instruction techniques, upcoming meetings and conferences, and recently posted job listings. Discussion lists also allow you to ask work-related questions to an audience that will likely be able to answer you.

Joining a discussion list is known as 'subscribing' and is generally straightforward, but varies by list. To leave a list, you must 'unsubscribe.' Most lists give several options for receiving the messages sent to the group. We recommend that you receive a digest of the day's messages, particularly for high-volume lists. The digest is a single e-mail that contains all the day's messages. Most lists use the digest as their default method of sending messages. You can also choose to receive messages as soon as they are sent to the list. However, this method of delivery can cause your e-mail inbox to overflow, as each message will be sent individually, no matter how trivial.

A list may be moderated by a list owner. This person decides whether a message submitted to the listserv should be copied and sent to the whole group. The list owner prevents e-mails not related to the topic of the list from being distributed to the group. Some lists have no moderator. In this case, members must police themselves.

You may be automatically subscribed to discussion lists for your library, institution, and/or scholarly society. If you are looking for additional lists to join, first ask your colleagues for recommendations. Another good source is *CataList*, 'the official catalog of LISTSERV® lists' (*http://www.lsoft.com/lists/listref.html*).

## *Journals*

Like other disciplines, library science relies heavily upon academic and trade journals to share information on the field. There are numerous titles devoted to the profession as a whole as well as those that look at a particular subfield such as reference, collection development, and serials. There are also journals that focus on specific types of libraries such as school libraries, public libraries, academic libraries, and special libraries. Scanning the literature will allow you to keep abreast of the changes in the field, regardless of your specialty.

Set aside some time regularly to browse journal literature. Once a month, visit the periodicals section of your library to browse the table of contents of your favorite journals. If your library has a good collection of online library journals, you can browse the literature from your computer. You will probably get your academic society's journal for 'free' as a perk of membership. Read it. Also consider signing up for the table of contents services of your favorite journals, which can be delivered directly by e-mail.

## Non-library publications

News related to our profession is not just limited to library journals. Library- and information-related stories often appear in popular magazines and newspapers. Outside perspectives of topics in our field such as digital publishing or censorship can be illuminating. Keep your eyes open for such stories.

Here are some publications that occasional carry library stories:

- *The Chronicle of Higher Education*. Although this publication is geared towards university administrators, it also covers information technology and funding issues in libraries.

- *The New York Times, Time magazine, and other national newspapers and news magazines*. About once a week, there is a story on some aspect of libraries in the national news. Sign up for news tracker services that notify you by e-mail anytime an interesting story is published.

- *Your local paper, and institutional newsletters and/or research magazines.* These publications will have stories that are of immediate interest to your patrons (and, by extension, to you).

- *Subject-specialized journals and magazines.* Particularly if you deal with a specific group of faculty and students, you will need to keep up with the information technologies of interest in your field. This is often called the 'informatics' of a discipline.

EBSCO Academic Search Elite, ABI/INFORM, Proquest and LexisNexis Academic provide a wealth of articles from library journals.

## Meetings and conferences

Although they are discussed in detail elsewhere in the book, attending meetings and conferences are great ways to stay current with the state of the art in libraries. They afford you opportunities to discover how other libraries and librarians have handled problems common to all in the field. They offer you the chance to network with other librarians, which can be especially useful in future job searches. Your library may subsidize a portion of the expenses associated with traveling to and attending meetings and conferences.

# Conclusion

In this chapter we hope we have changed the way you think about your communication skills and that we have given you some resources that will keep you current in the profession. You could put the two together and figure out how to use your communication skills to share what you have learned with your colleagues. Good communication is also, at its best, a time-saver. When you don't have to do a lot of explaining, work can move faster toward completion.

## Further reading

Bradley, Jana and Bradley, Larry (1998) *Improving Written Communication in Libraries*. Chicago: American Library Association.

Brounstein, Marty (2001) *Business Etiquette for Dummies*. Foster City, CA: IDG Books.

Cohen, Allan and Bradford, David (1990) *Influence Without Authority*. New York: John Wiley & Sons.

Conroy, Barbara and Jones, Barbara S. (1986) *Improving Communication in the Library*. Phoenix, AZ: Oryx Press.

Fox, Susan and Cunningham, Perrin (2001) *Communicating Effectively for Dummies*. New York: Hungry Minds.

Hamlin, Sonya (1988) *How to Talk So People Listen*. New York: Harper & Row.

Kaye, Ellen (2002) *Maximize Your Presentation Skills: How to Speak, Look and Act on Your Way to the Top*. Roseville, CA: Prima Publishing.

Kratz, Abby and Flannery, Melinda (1997) 'Communication skills,' in Joan Giesecke (ed.), *Practical Help for New Supervisors*. Chicago: American Library Association.

Levy, Philippa and Usherwood, Bob (1992) *People Skills: Interpersonal Training for Library and Information Work.* London: British Library Board.

McKay, Matthew and Fanning, Patrick (1995) *Messages: The Communication Skills Book.* Oakland, CA: New Harbinger Publications.

Riggs, Donald E. (ed.) (1991) *Library Communication: The Language of Leadership.* Chicago: American Library Association.

Ross, Catherine Sheldrick and Dewdney, Patricia (1998) *Communication Professionally: A How-to-do-it Manual for Library Applications*, 2nd edn. New York: Neal-Schuman Publishers.

Sabin, William A. (2000) *The Gregg Reference Manual.* New York: McGraw-Hill/Irwin.

Scheuermann, Larry and Taylor, Gary (1997) 'Netiquette,' *Internet Research*, 7, 4: 269–73.

Strunk, William and White, E.B. (2000) *The Elements of Style*, 4th edn. New York: Longman.

Sturges, Paul (2002) 'Remember the human: the first rule of netiquette, librarians and the Internet,' *Online Information Review*, 26, 3: 209–16.

Ury, William (1991) *Getting Past No: Negotiating With Difficult People.* New York: Bantam.

# Meetings

*Life is a continuous exercise in creative problem solving.*

Michael J. Gelb

Academic libraries have long used committees and task forces for cross-departmental projects or to start new ventures to move the progress of the library forward. Many librarians think that this type of work is not something they need to focus their energy on. This is a mistake. Much of the work that an academic library does takes place in committees, and it is a responsibility of all academic librarians to take that work seriously.

If you are a typical academic librarian, your daily schedule contains more than just a few meetings. Some are with fellow librarians, some with faculty or students, and some with your boss or other administrators. In this chapter we focus heavily on what your roles and responsibilities are as a meeting participant, and what your roles and responsibilities are as the chair or leader of a group. Next is a discussion of some of the different kinds of meetings (including electronic and interviewing meetings) that you can expect in an academic library. We conclude with a section on how to take good minutes. Sometimes, if you are not aware of it, your minutes will reveal more about you or someone else than what actually happened at the meeting. Minutes can be a political pitfall. We show you how to write minutes that share the important details about what happened without getting anyone in hot water.

## Meetings are work

Meetings are not intrusions on your schedule – they are part and parcel of your work. They are just as important to the organization as that reference question you just answered, or that serial you just cataloged. Libraries are faced with constant change, and the work we do is increasingly dependent on the work of other departments. Meetings are how things get done beyond the scope of individuals and their departments or divisions.

A meeting is not necessarily a formal gathering of important people. It can be as simple as two or more people getting together, face-to-face, on the phone, or electronically, to work toward a common goal – either their own or one that they were charged with carrying out. There are several types and formats of meetings, but they all have one thing in common. Meetings facilitate the work of different people, groups, and units so that the library functions as a cohesive entity.

## Responsibilities of meeting attendees

You've been asked to serve on a task group – so what now? Before you attend the first meeting, prepare yourself by reading the charge, thinking about your skills and experience, and brainstorming how you can help. As a meeting participant, you have certain roles and responsibilities. These include:

- sharing your expertise;

- making sure the group's work is accomplished, and done well;

- learning how what you do relates to what other departments do in the library;

- thinking of the library as a body that won't function without cooperation and improvement. No organ (or department) is more important than any other.

In addition, as a participant you have responsibilities that extend beyond the systemic ones listed above. These are discussed in more detail below.

## Go to all meetings

It's amazing that we have to include this point, but years of experience have shown that this seeming no-brainer is a difficult concept for some people. Put the meeting on your schedule and show up *on time or slightly early*. If you have a conflict, immediately contact the chair and let him or her know. Ask what you will miss. Volunteer to do some other work for the group to atone. Most of the time you won't be asked to do anything. By offering, you will be seen as taking part even if you don't make it to a meeting or two.

### Be prepared

Read the agenda and any preparatory information before the meeting. Bring copies with you to the meeting. If you have an assignment from a previous meeting, be prepared to talk about it. Share the results with the rest of the group. Don't waste precious meeting time catching up with everyone else.

### Find your role

What role do you naturally fall into in groups? Are you an information gatherer, a brainstorming ideas person, or a report writer? Figure out what role(s) you can play in each group and volunteer to do the activities relative to those roles. Don't limit yourself. If you find yourself getting tired of doing the same old thing in every group, volunteer to do something new. Tell the group leader you would like to learn a new skill. Ask him or her for guidance if you feel you will need it.

### Facilitate!

It is the job of every member of the group to help move the work forward. Learn some facilitation skills in order to do your part well. One of the best things you can do to facilitate the action is to lose your ego. Nietzsche said it best when he said: '...I am followed by a dog called "Ego".' Don't take *anything* personally. Remember, it is all about work – not about you personally! Your selflessness will push your career and your library's work faster than your ego ever could.

# Responsibilities of meeting leaders

## *Expectations and respect*

Members of every group have expectations of the person or person running the meeting. If you are that person and don't fulfill their expectations, you will not get their full appreciation or commitment to the work of the group. These expectations generally include:

- that you will have a clear understanding of, and be able to articulate to the members of the group, the reason(s) that you are all meeting. You have to know the charge inside and out so that you are able to explain it;

- that you will run each meeting in an organized, forward-moving manner, and share all group-related information in a timely fashion;

- that you will provide them with, or point them to, the resources they will need to carry out their duties for the group;

- that you will be able to facilitate the meetings *specifically* so that strong personalities don't take over and weak personalities don't get lost;

- that you will help each person use his or her strengths to reach the goals of the group.

These are some heavy responsibilities, yes. But think about it: if you are a member in a group where the leader does not fulfill these expectations, are you not unhappy and demoralized? Haven't you lost the respect for the group and its leader? So when you are the chair, think hard about your role and the expectations of the people you are leading.

## Form the charge

No group can get anything done unless the members of the group have a clear understanding of the answers to certain questions:

- What is the group's purpose? Why are we meeting?
- What is the timeline for meetings, reporting, or project completion?
- What are our final products?
- Who do we report to?
- What will be done with the work we do?

If the answers are not clear at the outset, the group will spend a lot of valuable time together trying to figure them out. It is the responsibility of each group member to ask these questions at the outset of the very first meeting. If you are not clear about the answers to any of these questions, you, as the chair, need to go back to whoever initiated the group (usually someone in administration) and ask them to answer those questions for you.

If you find that the group you are working with has lost its direction, then you, as a group member, need to stop the work of the group and ask for clarification. Revisit the charge and see if your work is applicable to what the charge is asking you to do. Ask:

- Are we responding to our original charge?
- Are our outcomes what we have been asked to do?
- Has the charge changed with time?
- Is this the right group of people to carry out this work?
- Does the charge need to be revisited to get people back on track?

The boundaries of the charge expressly guide the work of any group. If your charge is unclear, your work will be unfocused, and, in time, not useful to the institution.

## Set the agenda

Agendas have multiple purposes. They help people know ahead of time what to expect at a meeting so that they can prepare. They keep the meeting focused on the time and on moving forward. They provide a framework for the minute-taker. Lastly, they give everyone an opportunity to bring their issues to the table in a formalized manner. There are many different types of agendas, but most of them have the same key elements:

- Organizational information, including:
  - name of the group;
  - time, day, and place of the meeting;
  - meeting leader/committee chair;

- minute-taker/secretary/clerk.
- Items for discussion in the meeting, including:
  - announcements;
  - approval of the previous minutes;
  - agenda items – be realistic, and keep these to a number the group can get through in the time allotted;
  - other business – always allow people the opportunity to talk about relevant issues at the end of the meeting, if there is time.

Send out a preliminary agenda – including requests for agenda items – in plenty of time to give people the opportunity to respond with suggestions. Include with the final agenda any materials to be discussed so that people can arrive prepared. If you do this, people can use the meeting time to discuss what is on the agenda, and not spend time reading the handouts. Bring extra copies of any documents under discussion to the meeting, as some participants will inevitably forget theirs.

Plan agendas carefully. You are estimating how long each discussion will take. Be reasonable. There are a few factors to consider when thinking about planning your agendas. It is especially important to consider the personalities of the members. If someone is talkative and takes a long time to get to the point, it may be useful to put them at the end of the agenda. That way they will only have a small amount of time to talk before the meeting is over. Group pressure will force them to stick to the point and keep it brief, because as the end of the meeting approaches, people get tired and restless.

When inviting non-members to your meeting, decide when will be the best time for them to attend. They probably will not want, nor have the time, to sit through the parts of your meeting in which they are not involved. Decide whether they should come at the beginning and then leave after the group has talked with them, or at the end so that the meeting can end after their topic is discussed.

## Establish group norms

One of the ways to keep the work of the group running smoothly is to create ground rules or group norms for behavior. It is important that they originate from the group, so that members take them seriously. Some organizations have institutional norms for its committees and groups. These can go a long way toward helping a group get its work done. One note: while ground rules are especially useful for task groups and short-term groups that need to get a lot of work done in a finite amount of time, longer-standing groups can also benefit from the creation of ground rules.

Ground rules are process statements that the group creates together. These statements list how the group will govern their time and activities in a meeting. They keep a group from getting bogged down in dealing with group dynamics and the bad behavior of individual members.

Probably one of the best ways to set up ground rules is to start with a prepared list. Have the group alter it so that the rules work for everyone involved. Below is a sample ground rules list, taken loosely from the *Facilitator's Fieldbook* (Justice and Jamieson, 1999: 73–4):

- Sessions start on time. We will not review the discussion for latecomers.
- Phone messages will be delivered at breaks except for personal emergencies.
- One person talks at a time.
- What is said here stays here.
- If you miss any session, support the decision made in your absence.
- Listen first as an advocate for the other person's idea.
- Every idea and comment is valid.
- People need not agree.
- All data is recorded on flip charts.
- All tasks have recorded outputs.
- We stick to the time allotted for discussion.
- Meetings are not a lecture forum.

# Meeting types

## Informative or reporting meetings

Informative or reporting meetings are held by groups of which you are a member by virtue of your position and place in the library. For the most part, these meetings are less about getting lots of work done than about sharing information you need to do your job. Also they are for soliciting feedback and ideas about larger library issues. A common example of this meeting type is your regular departmental meeting.

## Working meetings

You will be chosen or may volunteer to be a member of most committees, task groups, or work groups to which you belong. These groups meet to accomplish a task, whether it is planning or executing a project, or editing results. You are there because you have some knowledge or expertise that is seen as useful to the work of that particular group.

## Interviews

Interviews are a blend of the two types of meetings discussed above. You may attend an open session or be part of a small group asked to meet with job candidates. On the one hand, you are receiving information about the candidates, and providing information to them about yourself and your organization. On the other hand, you have a decision-influencing role as a participant in the interview process. Your responsibilities in interviews are similar to other types of meetings, with some specific tasks:

- Read the candidate's CV before meeting him or her.
- Do your homework concerning the person's background, including reading anything that the candidate may have published in journals or publications, conducting a search for him or her on the Internet, and reviewing their current position.

- Prepare questions to ask the candidate.

- After the interview, prepare a report (sometimes a form is provided) for the selection committee.

### Electronic meetings

Much group work can be handled via e-mail, especially if candidates are dispersed geographically. With a few simple guidelines, e-mail meetings can make the work of the group that much more efficient.

Guidelines for e-mail meetings may include:

- Any group work or discussion will be sent to the entire group. No one will be excluded.

- Only the portion of the e-mail that is being responded to will be included in the response to it.

- Responses will be timely. If you haven't responded within the group's set time limit, you have lost your chance to respond. This keeps people from rehashing decisions that have already been decided by the larger majority.

- Get together physically every once in a while to make sure everyone is on track.

- Assign one person keeper of all of the group's e-mails as a record of the work.

## Writing up meeting minutes

Recording a meeting is not as straightforward as it seems. Because accountability, timeliness, and organizational politics are often involved with writing up the minutes, it can make your job as minute-taker quite tricky. Consider the following issues if this delicate task falls on your shoulders.

## The nuts and bolts of taking minutes

- Make sure you record the obvious information like the date, the names of those who attended the meeting, and the names of those who were absent.

- Go prepared with plenty of pens and paper so you won't have to rely on your memory to recap the meeting. Some people use their laptop computers to record the minutes. This speeds along the sending out of the minutes, since you don't have to spend time later transcribing your written notes into a word processing file. If you do choose to use a laptop, make sure the typing noise doesn't upset any of the meeting participants.

- Don't be afraid to stop the meeting and ask for clarification on a point. You don't want to write down notes that don't make sense to you. Often, other participants at the meeting might be just as confused as you are, so they will appreciate further explanation.

- If you find yourself always taking the minutes, suggest to the group that minute-taking be rotated among the meeting's participants. Nobody need always be stuck with this task.

## Accountability and politics

- There are probably many hot issues in your library, such as rivalries between departments and funding shortages.

Be careful when you write about these divisive topics in your minutes. Try to adopt a neutral tone in your writing. You might also ask the group, 'This seems like a delicate topic. How shall I write it in the minutes?'

- Don't list the names of speakers in your minutes. Often, what is said in meetings is meant for a limited audience. When writing minutes, you might actually want to use the passive voice. So instead of writing 'the assistant director said...', you could write 'it was said...'. Doing this allows meeting participants to speak openly in heated discussions without fear of repercussion.

- Be certain that you list any tasks that must be performed by the group in the minutes. This will let all of the participants know who is responsible for any actions. In turn this helps create accountability in the group or committee. You can mark these action statements by listing them separately at the end of the document, or by highlighting them in bold if you leave them as statements embedded in the text.

## After the meeting is finished

- Make sure you send out the minutes in a timely manner. Many times a group will have a deadline as to when minutes must go out. Don't be like minute-takers that the authors know who will wait up to six months before sending out their minutes. By that time the information does no one any good. We leave it up to you to figure out what your colleagues think of those who act this way.

- If the meeting participants are to give you feedback before sending out the minutes, give them a deadline. Let them know you will send out the minutes after a specified time whether you hear back from them or not. Experience has proven that meekly waiting for all meeting attendees to respond to minute corrections will leave you hanging out to dry and, horror of horrors, publishing your minutes six months later!

## Conclusion

Meetings can be terribly exciting and fast-paced experiences, but only if the group members let them. Learning how to make meetings work can make your entire work life change. One of the authors remembers fondly meetings of a task force on digital library planning that actually got her so excited that she would leave the meetings raring to go. Even now, she runs into fellow members of that same group, and every one of them had the same reaction. We hope that by using some of the skills we have discussed in this chapter, you too will have exciting meetings.

## Further reading

Amos, Julie-Ann (2000) *Making Meetings Work*. Oxford: Essentials.

Barry, David (1991) 'Managing the bossless team: lessons in distributed leadership,' *Organizational Dynamics*, 20, 1: 31–47.

Brewerton, Antony W. (2002) 'How to virtually enjoy meetings,' *Library Association Record*, 104, 2: 104–5.

Burleson, Clyde W. (1990) *Effective Meetings: The Complete Guide*. New York: John Wiley & Sons.

Dewey, Barbara I. and Creth, Shelia D. (1993) *Team Power: Making Library Meetings Work*. Chicago: American Library Association.

Grudin, Robert (1990) *The Grace of Great Things: Creativity and Innovation*. New York: Ticknor & Fields.

Haynes, Marion and Crisp, Michael G. (eds) (1998) *Effective Meeting Skills* (rev. edn). Menlo Park, CA: Crisp Publications.

Howard, V.A. and Barton, J.H. (1986) *Thinking Together: Making Meetings Work*. New York: Morrow.

Justice, Thomas and Jamieson, David (1999) *The Facilitator's Fieldbook: Step-by-Step Procedures, Checklists and Guidelines, Samples and Templates*. New York: AMACOM Books.

McCallister, Myrna Joy and Paterson, Thomas H. (1997) 'Conducting effective meetings,' in Joan Giesecke (ed.), *Practical Help for New Supervisors*. Chicago: American Library Association.

Maier, N. (1970) *Problem Solving and Creativity in Individuals and Groups*. Belmont, CA: Brooks/Cole.

Mina, Eli (2000) *The Complete Handbook of Business Meetings*. New York: AMACOM Books.

Mosvick, Roger K. and Nelson, Robert B. (1997) *We've Got to Start Meeting Like This: A Guide to Successful Meeting Management*. Indianapolis, IN: Jist Works.

Murphy, Amy and Ashmore, Beth (2002) 'Mia in the conference room,' *College and Undergraduate Libraries*, 9, 1: 19–22.

Randall, Robert J. and Englund, Randall L. (1997) *Creating an Environment for Successful Projects: The Quest to Manage Project Management*. San Francisco: Jossey-Bass.

Tagliere, Daniel A. (1993) *How to Meet, Think and Work to Consensus*. San Diego, CA: Pfeiffer.

Timm, Paul R. (1997) *How to Hold Successful Meetings: 30 Action Tips for Managing Effective Meetings*, 30 Minute Solutions Series. Franklin Lakes, NJ: Career Press.

Tropman, John E. (2003) *Making Meetings Work: Achieving High Quality Group Decisions*. Thousand Oaks, CA: Sage Publications.

Wanden, Joy A. (2001) 'Making meetings matter!', *Library Mosaics*, 12, 4: 8–12.

Young, Bonnie (2002) 'Benefits of using an unchanging agenda at library staff meetings,' *Public Libraries*, 41, 5: 241–2.

# 6

# Collection development in an electronic world

*Give me the strength to change the things I can, the grace to accept the things I cannot, and a great big bag of money.*

Jack Handey

Collection development (CD) in an electronic world – and this is one of the only two library-centric chapters included. Why? Real-world CD is hard to teach in school. On a practical level it is often more about people and collaboration than it is about building a collection. Most likely the collection is already built at your library and you are just carrying on from the previous person who collected in that area. Technology plays a much larger role than in the past. The service aspect of collection-building and managing becomes ever more important in times of tight budgets and ever-increasing costs. Further, gathering and making sense of information from vendors, other librarians, the collections, and users themselves becomes vital to the work of CD. In this chapter, we hope to give you a good framework of things to do, look out for, and consider as you delve into your CD work.

# Technology skills

Collection development is now about technology almost as much as it is about content. If you do not have a strong handle on the technology, you will not be able to do your CD well. You have to be able to test new products, create Web pages for products and projects, compare and analyze new and existing products, and use mailing lists to share information about products you may, or may not yet, own.

## Testing products – new and existing

> To be intelligent is to be open-minded, active, memoried, and persistently experimental.
>
> Leopold Stein

A significant portion of a library budget goes toward the purchase of and subscription to electronic materials: databases, electronic journals, and electronic books. Before you buy, and even after you already own these products, you will find that there is a great need to test their value and to review them in order to change titles or cancel them altogether.

## Elements for testing

Below are a number of lists to get you started. We are sure you will come up with criteria of your own as you gain more experience or find other needs for the information.

## Price

- What is its cost relative to similar options?
- What is the cost per full-time equivalent (FTE) or potential user?
- How many user 'seats' will you need? How many can you afford?
- Will you need to have access for the entire campus, or only a small user group?
- How much will it cost to add users in the future?

## Duplication

- What is the coverage (journal titles, years of coverage, full text, etc.)?
- How easy is it to find the publication lists? Do they actually have what they claim they have?
- Does this title duplicate or overlap significantly with something you already own or subscribe to?

## Ease of use

- Is the interface easy to figure out? Will you have to spend a significant amount of time teaching users how to use it? Is it so confusing that it won't get used at all?
- Would it be worthwhile waiting until they improve it?
- Is there another vendor who offers access to the same information, and, if so, is it easier to use?

- How responsive are the vendor contacts when you request information?
- Does the search interface allow advanced or guided use?

### Using technology to reach your users

You will need to be comfortable enough with technology that you can interact with your users via e-mail and the Web. You can create tools on the Web to manage review projects, to market new materials, and to explain to users how to use products. Use e-mail to alert your users to changes or problems in electronic material access, to solicit their feedback on review projects, and to keep them informed about what is new, and what is being cancelled.

Creating a newsletter is often a terrific way to interact with your users. Remember to keep it short, timely, and focused on things that they need to know now or in the near future. If they know that it is direct and full of information they need, they will read it. If feasible, you can also send a paper form of the e-mail newsletter. In addition, if your library has a message board, you can post the newsletter.

## Using electronic mailing lists – what is good, what isn't, information sharing

Almost every niche of library science has its own mailing lists. These online groups are invaluable for a variety of reasons, and are available in all aspects of academic librarianship. They are especially useful for gathering up-to-date information about products you are thinking about buying, or products you are reviewing for cancellation. To quickly find one in the area you collect in, use your favorite web search engine and search for 'library listservs.' These groups of like-minded colleagues can be invaluable to your CD work. Don't hesitate to post questions about products to the list. However, this is not a good location to send nasty complaints about products to. Be fair, but direct. If something doesn't work well, say so. However, remember e-mail can have a life of its own. And anything you write in an e-mail to a large group of people ultimately reflects back on the writer. For more information about how to find and use lists, look in Chapter 4 on communication.

## Public service

> I can't change the direction of the wind, but I can adjust my sails to always reach my destination.
>
> Jimmy Dean

Every aspect of library work has a public service component. Many academic libraries have public service and CD tied into the same position. Other libraries have separate positions for these two activities. No matter how your library is organized, you can be sure that if you are doing CD, you will be doing public service. There's no way around it. If you are selecting materials to satisfy the needs of your library's users, you will interact with these users. For a more in-depth discussion on service issues, look in Chapter 7.

## Liaison

*The American Heritage Dictionary* (second edition) defines liaison as 'communication between different groups or units in an organization.' As a liaison for CD you will share information with and gather information from any library user who is interested in a subject area or areas in which you collect. You will need to:

- Make yourself known and available to these people – it is especially important to make it *easy* for them to find and contact you.

- Communicate with them via e-mail, personal visits, etc. to build their trust in your skills and knowledge.

- Find out their research interests, and stay up-to-date with changes in research emphasis at the departmental, as well as the individual level.

## Marketing

Because libraries are still in the transition phase of incorporating electronic information products into the mainstream of library resources, it is often very confusing to users what we do or do not have available. Not everything is listed in the library catalog. Sometimes users have to go to multiple resources to find all of the appropriate materials they may need for their research, such as the catalog, a list of databases, a list of electronic journals, and a sign posted somewhere, etc.

We have a fiscal responsibility, as well as a service responsibility, to make sure our users know what we have. For example, when one of the authors began at a new university a while ago, she discovered that the library was paying for a service that at the time was called UnCover. Its main value to researchers was that it e-mailed tables of contents for recently published journals in a large variety of subjects. After looking at the use statistics, the author realized no one was using it. Why? Because the library's patrons didn't know the library had it. What a waste of a few thousand dollars! She decided that the library needed to let people know this service was available. So she and her staff undertook a multi-pronged marketing program: they created a brochure that would be printed up and sent to all faculty and many graduate students on what UnCover was and how to set it up. A stack of these pamphlets was also kept at the reference and circulation desks. Finally, she alerted users to the service by highlighting it on the library's homepage. Copies are still sent to new faculty and are kept for people who come to the library for help. The 'campaign' made a big difference. Use of UnCover went up exponentially within a few short months. The library got a lot of good feedback on the product from faculty and graduate students. Marketing *can* make a difference.

The previous example demonstrates that marketing needs to incorporate as many different avenues as possible. Get creative and try all kinds of techniques, including:

- Have a 'new and noteworthy' section of the library newsletter.
- Put up table tents in the faculty or student lounge.
- Use targeted e-mails about resources of interest to specific faculty.

- Use mass e-mails to e-mail lists for resources of general interest.

- Post flyers, notices, etc. on the library doors or bulletin boards.

- Post announcements on the library website or homepage.

- Give away promotional materials (often available for free from the vendor).

- Teach classes or have an 'open house' for new products.

- Demonstrate products to library staff and users at a brown bag seminar.

Check out the resources at the end of this chapter for other ways to market library resources.

## Assessment and statistics

Assessment is key to the work of collection building and managing. It is very important to remember that physical contact is as good as and sometimes better than any statistical information. At every new job, try to spend time during the first few months physically walking the stacks and looking at the collection in your subject(s). Look for dust – this will often tell you what is or isn't being used. Look for materials that are falling apart. These could be old, or could have high use. Try to figure out what gets checked out, and what doesn't. This could change with different times of the year. Try to tie together what you see on the shelf with what you find out about the research people do at your university.

In large part, because of the exponential cost of collecting scholarly information, our role as collection managers and developers of academic library collections has migrated to one also of access providers. Because of the effect of monetary cuts on the buying power of our budgets, we are much more concerned with just-in-time (JIT) access to information rather than just-in-case archiving of books and journals. Only a few well-endowed libraries can create true research-level collections, and even those are in only a few very specific areas. Use drives collections. For some, this is a sad statement. In these times we have to be contentious money managers. We supply current users the materials they need now. Building for historical use is no longer monetarily feasible, nor a wise activity.

While this is not the venue to talk about the scholarly communication crisis, since others have waxed poetic on this subject, we are concerned with giving you suggestions and ideas on how you and your library users can cope with this new concept of what an academic collection is.

## Importance of gathering statistics

Use statistics are the primary tool for collection assessment. In this day and age, gathering and analyzing statistics on the use of library materials (both in print and electronic, and especially of serial materials) is a very important activity for anyone doing CD. One of your roles is that of justifier and explainer of your CD actions and decisions. This is especially difficult because you have very little if any control of the events that you must explain and then justify. By having statistics to back up your CD decisions, you will be able to have productive interactions with faculty, graduate students, and your fellow librarians. Explaining to your faculty and students the limitations you are under is easier when you have numbers to prove your point. Access in lieu of ownership is often an acceptable alternative once people understand the fiscal realities of libraries.

## Gathering statistics – make it part of the process

Incorporate the gathering of use statistics into an activity that already involves the action of these materials being used. Make tallying use part of the shelving process. Automate it if you can, with bar-code reading when the materials are reshelved, or by tallying at the point of sorting for shelving, or incorporate it into the shelving process itself. The ability to show the level of use any individual title received over any given period of time – constantly and forever – makes your job as a politician that much easier.

# Document delivery as collection development

Another tool available to you to counter shrinking budgets is interlibrary loan, now more often called 'document delivery.' You can and should consider document delivery/interlibrary loan as a part of collection management. While many will disagree with us, we believe libraries no longer have the budgets at hand to sustain the dynamic growth of scholarly publication and the infusion of the for-profit publishing world into scholarly publishing. If document delivery works well, then having the materials on-site becomes less important for the users. Actually, many of them don't really care whether the library owns it or not. As long as you can get it for them, their needs have been met. And isn't it really about meeting the needs of our users?

Academic libraries are redefining who and what they are. What does being a librarian mean? Now that people can find lots of information on the Internet, what is our role and responsibility to the user? What do our users expect of us? In the academic world, our users increasingly see us as procurers of information for them. Because we cannot own everything, we have to get more and more stuff for them. It is not necessarily bad, it is just different.

So how does that change the work of the librarian? Collection management and development becomes an activity with a very strong public service component. It is almost collection and access management. You need to have a strong, close relationship with your users. They have to trust you and know who you are, in order for you to fulfill your role. Liaison activities have become tantamount to succeeding in collection development. These skills are similar to the previous ones of knowing publishers and vendors, but have expanded into knowing also how to help your users get the material for their one-time use from somewhere else.

## Vendors and publishers

Dealing with vendors and publishers can be very simple, as long as you keep the following dos and don'ts in mind:

- *Do* remember that not only are the vendors out to make money, the person on the other end of the line probably makes a commission off his sales. It's not your job to put food on the tables of people who sell databases!

- *Don't* take cold calls from vendors. Listen to your users, not the sellers, when deciding what to buy. Tell the vendors, 'send me the info, and I'll call you when I am ready.'

- *Do* set up a demonstration *and* a trial period for every new electronic package, whether you are seriously considering it or not. Make sure your users know about the demo and the trial, and solicit feedback from them about it.

- *Don't* buy products that aren't ready for prime time. Tell the vendor that they need to improve it before you will buy it. If you do buy it and it is unacceptable, no one will use it. Not only will you have spent money on a poor product, you will have to spend more money and bargaining power for a replacement. In addition, vendors rarely improve a product in which people have already invested. If it has already been sold, what incentive do they have to improve it?

- *Do* give constructive criticism about a product to the vendor's representative. Companies will sometimes go to great lengths to improve a product so that you will buy it or extend your licence.

# Licensing electronic materials

## *Educate yourself on the issues and the criteria of licences*

Most likely your library will have someone on staff who is responsible for handling the nitty-gritty details of licences. However, in your role as a collection developer, it is important that you are aware of the issues involved with licensing and are an extra set of eyes reviewing the agreements. You may need to share licensing information with your users, since many agreements cover use of materials as well as price. The section on marketing earlier in this chapter suggests some tips that will be helpful here as well.

You also need to know any restrictions on licences due to the law and/or policies of your own institution and state, province, or country. These will all have an effect on what kind of licence you can or cannot sign.

The time that it takes to negotiate and sign licences can have an impact on you and your users. It can take longer than a year to get a license agreement on which both the library and the vendor can agree. During this time you may have faculty and graduate students clamoring at your door and sending you e-mails asking you where this product is. You may have to explain the whole licensing process to them. It is probably a good idea to have a statement about licensing on your web page, or at least in a handy paper format to share this kind of information with library users. If your library does not have one, write up a sample one and advocate getting it finalized and incorporated into the library's policies and procedures page so that what the faculty and students are told will be the same university-wide.

## Conclusion

The only way to really do CD well is to keep educating yourself on what is possible. It can be a fantastic opportunity to interact with people who use the library and there is no better way to keep up with what is going on in the world. Keep in mind you are buying for the library user and you will not go wrong.

## Further reading

Abel, Richard E. and Newlin, Lyman W. (eds) (2002) *Scholarly Publishing: Books, Journals, Publishers, and Libraries in the Twentieth Century*. New York: Wiley.

Borgman, Christine L. (2000) *From Gutenberg to the Global Information Infrastructure: Access to Information in the Networked World*. Cambridge, MA: MIT Press.

Fowler, David C. (2003) *E-Serials Collection Management: Transitions, Trends, and Technicalities*. Binghamton, NY: Haworth Information Press.

Harris, Lesley Ellen (2002) *Licensing Digital Content: A Practical Guide for Librarians*. Chicago: American Library Association.

Jones, Wayne (2003) *E-Serials: Publishers, Libraries, Users, and Standards*. New York: Haworth Information Press.

Lee, Stuart D. (2002) *Electronic Collection Development: A Practical Guide*. New York: Neal-Schuman Publishers.

Lee, Sul H. (2002) *Electronic Resources and Collection Development*. New York: Haworth Information Press.

*Lib-License: Licensing Digital Information, A Resource for Librarians*. Yale University; available online at: *http://www.library.yale.edu/~llicense/*.

McGinnis, Susan (ed.) (2000) *Electronic Collection Development*. New York: Haworth Information Press.

Rupp-Serrano, Karen (2000) *Collection Management: Preparing Today's Bibliographers for Tomorrow's Libraries*. New York: Haworth Press.

De Saez, Eileen Elliott (2002) *Marketing Concepts for Libraries and Information Services*, 2nd edn. London: Facet Publishing.

Schwartz, Peter (1991) *The Art of the Long View: Planning for the Future in an Uncertain World*. New York: Doubleday.

Wiggins, Gary (1992) 'Collection development vs. access in academic science libraries,' in Cynthia A. Steinke (ed.), *Sci-Tech Libraries of the Future*. New York: Haworth Press.

# 7

# Public service in the electronic world

Change has a considerable psychological impact on the human mind. To the fearful it is threatening because it means that things may get worse. To the hopeful it is encouraging because things may get better. To the confident it is inspiring because the challenge exists to make things better.

King Whitney Jr

This chapter is one of two in this book that is focused on an especially library-centric role. Here we are primarily concerned with defining major changes in the librarian's public service role, and with discussing specifically what you need to do to meet the changing needs and expectations of library patrons. The growth of electronic resources has greatly affected how users perform their library research. More importantly, users' perception of the library, and of librarians, has changed. To meet the challenges of the electronic environment, you must be willing to acquire new skills to provide new services. In particular, you need to cultivate proficiencies in multiple formats for managing your reference and electronic collections.

## Roles change as resources change

Most libraries are making an increasingly larger percentage of their collections available electronically. For instance, the Duke University Libraries had subscriptions to 11,850 electronic journals and more than 300 research databases in 2003. With more publishers putting their titles online, and with space a growing concern, emphasis on electronic resources will continue into the future. Stating that these electronic resources will change public services is obvious, but describing these changes is not so straightforward. Issues of archiving, budgeting, title cancellation, and space will most likely be involved. However, in this chapter we are primarily interested in what you as an academic librarian must do to meet the changing needs and expectations of users. Electronic resources affect how the public performs library research, as well as their perception of the library as more of the print collection becomes available online. To meet the challenges of this electronic environment, you must be willing to acquire new skills and provide new services. You must become proficient in electronic collections management and further your commitment to public service. If you don't, your users will change without you.

> If you put garbage in a computer nothing comes out but garbage. But this garbage, having passed through a very expensive machine, is somehow ennobled and none dare criticize it.
>
> Anonymous

# What skills do you need to have?

## *Reference skills*

Just as the resources themselves are changing, the opportunities to use those resources and communicate the changes are expanding. You now have many more channels with which to communicate with your patrons than were available only five years ago. Whether you plan to or not, you will be providing reference services to library users not only in the traditional face-to-face method, but also over the telephone, via e-mail, and increasingly using one of the many online chat software packages. Because it is (one hopes) easier for users to reach you without actually coming into the library, it can feel like you are answering e-mails and the telephone all day long. Keep in mind that your job is to help your public – so you are *not* being interrupted by these questions. They're what you're there for!

You will need to develop certain skills to keep up with managing reference services in the digital age. Most critical are remote reference skills. Since an increasing number of students and faculty do their research from some location away from the library – and possibly off-campus altogether – expecting that they will come into the library to find an answer may be unrealistic. Instead, you will need to cultivate skills in transferring information over the telephone or the computer that you would normally expect the patron to read for himself. Skills that are particularly useful are typing, e-mail and telephone etiquette (see Chapter 4 on communication), multitasking, and troubleshooting of electronic problems. Basic reference skills, however, stay constant regardless of format – these include the primacy of the reference interview, listening, and follow-through.

Just-in-time reference supports the independent, self-sufficient user. How do you offer the best service to the majority of your library users? Create finding aids that are easy to use, clear, and available in multiple formats and styles. Web publishing skills, including facility with an HTML editor or hand-coding, are skills that are necessary for your toolbox. You will also need to produce print finding aids, including pathfinders and other resource guides. Consider library signage to be a finding aid. Librarians need to study how to create good signage in order to make the library more accessible. Being able to publish professional documents – whether online or in print – is an extremely valuable skill that will help you tremendously in your public service career.

## Instruction skills

Teaching your users how information is organized in a highly structured electronic environment is key to making sure that they are finding the information they need. Instruction skills that embrace course design, integration into the curricula, and web-based instruction are vital for public service librarians. You can't just sit back and assume that your patrons will figure out how to use the resources. You may decide to collaborate with faculty and instructors to ensure that your instruction is in line with what they are doing in the classroom. On-demand training modules that offer asynchronous instruction on basic topics such as database searching can reach audiences that you never see. It can also be helpful to think of each reference interaction as an opportunity for instruction. Think of the old adage, 'Give a man a fish, he eats for a day; teach a man to fish, he eats forever.' You will find that creating quick guides to basic resources that you can hand out at the reference desk (physical or virtual) help to teach people how to fish for information.

Instruction librarians are increasingly aware that their 'students' come from a wide range of demographic groups and skill sets. In one undergraduate class you may have both teenagers and older, nontraditional students. You could have students who have learning or physical disabilities. We are now recognizing that there are several major categories of learners, each with their own best style of learning. If you are doing instruction for the library, it is a good idea to brush up on the psychology of teaching and learning, including learning styles, needs hierarchies, interactivity, and other issues in course design.

> The real problem is not whether machines think but whether men do.
>
> B.F. Skinner

Here are some major issues that you might consider teaching to your users:

## The pros and cons of access

You can explain to your patrons – if they haven't already figured it out for themselves – that accessing the library will become easier as more electronic resources are acquired.

Most academic libraries allow users to access their online holdings around-the-clock and remotely, whether they are in their dorm, lab, office, or at home. As these resources continue to grow, patrons will spend less time making trips to physical libraries, leaving them more time for work in their office. Let your users know that it's not necessary to trek to the library when the library can come to them.

The bad news is that the abundance of electronic resources has created overlaps in journal coverage, which is confusing for your users. For example, the newsweekly *Time* can be accessed at Duke University through at least five different full-text databases. The journal *Chemical Week* can be accessed through four databases. Users now have these questions to consider:

■ What are the dates of coverage in the different databases?

■ Do the databases provide full or selective coverage?

■ Will the articles be presented as html text or as a pdf (or other format) full image?

After contemplating those questions (provided they even contemplate them at all) and choosing one access over another, users face an additional hurdle. They must now use an interface that is perhaps different from anything they have seen before. Only after familiarizing themselves with a new interface are they able to access their article. Some users will find this extra step easier than physically locating an article in the stacks and making a photocopy. Explaining these new considerations to users is part of your job as the number of electronic resources continues to expand.

## Consequences of the ease of use

One of the greatest benefits of electronic resources for your library patrons is their ease of use. Users can do a literature search in an online database in a fraction of the time it takes to perform the same search in a print equivalent. For example, if a user wants to find every article that cited a 1970 science paper, it would be necessary to search more than 30 volumes of the print *Science Citation Index*. Physically searching the volumes and copying down the desired citations could take hours. Performing the same search in the electronic equivalent, the *ISI Web of Science*, takes less than a minute. Results can be printed, e-mailed to the searcher's inbox, or saved to disk in a variety of formats (including one appropriate for citation management programs). Make sure your patrons aren't needlessly wasting their time with a print source if a comparable electronic one is available.

However, ease of use can come with its drawbacks. Because online databases are generally simpler and quicker to search, print indexes and abstracts are rarely used by patrons. If both print and electronic resources offered the same coverage, this would not pose a problem. However, print sources are often more comprehensive than their electronic equivalents, a fact most users don't consider. While users might be willing to sacrifice better coverage for ease of use by exclusively searching online sources, this trade-off can come with tragic consequences, as illustrated at Johns Hopkins University. A researcher at the medical school there, in an asthma study, limited his literature review to the

MEDLINE database, which indexes medical literature beginning in 1966. Had the researcher used *Index Medicus*, a print predecessor to MEDLINE, he would have found papers published in the 1950s that revealed the toxic effects of a chemical used in his study. The researcher's decision to rely only on the online database sacrificed not only completeness but also a healthy woman's life.[1]

## Academic integrity

The rise in electronic resources has affected our users' expectations of what we offer, and consequently what they will preferentially use. If users can get some of the collection electronically, then they want to get *all* of the collection electronically. Worse, they often avoid resources that aren't easily accessible. A mathematics professor admitted to us that he only reads journals that our library subscribes to electronically. This aversion to print has been seen by one of the authors in the citation lists of student papers she has graded. The undergraduates' bibliographies are dominated by articles that are easily accessible online. As students become accustomed to working electronically, you may find them citing fewer print-only sources. It is your responsibility to remind students that purposely avoiding print sources will result in poor scholarship. At the same time, many students report that they are required to photocopy the first page of print articles to prove that they are using 'non-Internet' sources. You may need to educate graduate student teaching assistants and faculty about the difference between the Web and the library's electronic resources. Refusing to allow students to use e-journals is just as dangerous a censorship issue as refusing to consider print resources in research.

## Savvy searching skills

Print indexes and abstracts utilize a search procedure that is generally transparent to your user. Searchers can easily tell whether they are searching an author or subject index simply by checking the page title. Electronic searching is not so straightforward. Often, searchers are confronted with a choice of multiple options such as a basic, advanced, or expert search. They can select to search numerous indexing fields, which can total over 20 for a single database. Many of these fields provide little relevancy to the search and often confuse the user. They must also decide which limits, if any, to use in their search. When finally they understand how to search one particular database, they have to begin all over again with their search in a different database. Good search results are limited by the user's understanding of how a particular database works. Too often users view databases as black boxes, where they enter search terms and hope some relevant results are returned. Even though many of your users are computer literate, you should expect to spend some time with them demonstrating the different databases and interfaces.

## E-resource support for distance education

You will soon discover that all your users are becoming distance learners, whether they live and work on campus or in a remote location. Electronic resources are naturally well-suited for distance learners. Scholarship no longer requires being tied to a physical place, as so much of the educational and research experience takes place electronically. Let your users know that electronic resources aid and enhance the growth of distance learning.

## Technical competencies

The need for public service librarians to be technologically savvy is greater than ever. You have to know what databases you have, and not only in your own specific subject areas. You have to be very comfortable with all varieties of search tools and the searching techniques appropriate to each. You need to have a very high comfort level with the basics of desktop computer support, and a thorough understanding of networking and proxy servers. Troubleshooting skills for software and hardware are necessary components of a librarian's toolkit. And finally, you must be willing to support electronic resources. It is what most, if not all, of your users prefer. If you try to steer them to a print source when there is an electronic source that does the same job, they will quickly get frustrated with what they will consider your poor public service attitude.

## Public relations skills

Since your library now has far more kinds of resources than even five years ago, and since you have more ways of reaching your patrons (and for them to reach you), you have to do more to let your users know what you have and how they can access it. Use any means necessary to share this type of information with them. The Duke Chemistry Library uses four main methods for advertising products to patrons: table tents, posters, flyers in user's mail boxes, and an irregularly issued e-mail newsletter titled *This Week in the Chemistry Library*. The e-newsletter follows this protocol: no more than two items per issue and, if at all possible, no more than one screen of information. Newsletters are sent out via e-mail to primary users as well as to a few secondary users. It is also printed out and posted on the front door of the library, and an archive is kept on the library's website.

There are some aspects of marketing and public relations that are specific to your public service roles. These focus on the uniqueness of the formats available and on the purpose of public service.

## Use every contact point

More and more library patrons never set foot in the library because they can get to most, if not all, of the materials they need from their office or home via their computers. This means that they will contact you over the telephone, via e-mail, or through a chat service for help rather than coming to the reference desk. Their needs will run from traditional reference questions to requests for assistance with technical aspects of connecting to online resources. Take advantage of your time on the telephone to mention the library's newest or coolest (if you want, but should be most cool!) service. Use the signature line of your e-mail to advertise your remote reference and instruction services. Have canned responses in your chat reference service that direct patrons to the library's newsletter or FAQs. Never let an opportunity to market the library pass you by!

### Educate!

Seize every opportunity to educate your users about the costs and licensing issues related to electronic resources, including impacts on the library's service capabilities. It is best to have a standard statement covering these areas to ensure that all users are given the same basic information. This will assuage their expectations, so that they remain realistic about what the library can afford and how long it can take a resource to wend its way through the licensing process. Savvy librarians do this early and often. Distance education students and faculty clamor for equal access to materials – which in the case of the patrons of a health sciences library, for example, could well save a life. However, providing excellent clinical tools is extremely costly, therefore the librarians make sure they present a balanced case to library patrons so that they are involved in making the hard choices about which library materials and services can be supported.

## Managing electronic resources

Managing electronic resources becomes a public services issue very quickly because libraries use management tools to organize their electronic holdings for both internal and external (public) use. These tools need to be searchable by type, title, subject, vendor, etc. Some libraries add databases into the online catalog to facilitate searching, but also keep separate, searchable lists to help users who are accessing resources remotely and to help librarians manage the resources. These lists sometimes merge into a 'database of databases' that can be a very powerful metasearching tool for users as well as a management system for the technical services staff. Keep in mind that electronic resources are not yet mainstreamed into most library systems. They are relatively new in the grand scheme of things, and are certain to undergo many changes before their management becomes business-as-usual.

Think about the following when managing electronic resources.

## Designate liaisons

Encourage your library to designate one person to work with specific publishers and vendors. This activity needs to be a major part of one person's job description. This person will be familiar with each vendor's history and response times. The vendors won't be called by multiple people from one library system, which confuses them. Instead, one person follows a problem or contract through from start to finish, and sends out vendor alerts. This is vital to public service management of e-resources. You may be the vendor liaison, particularly if you are the collection management person in a specific subject area or discipline.

## Keep statistics

Before electronic resources, libraries had to use a variety of inelegant methods to find out how, and how often, print resources were used. Be prepared to analyze how users use electronic materials in comparison to their print counterparts. Reviewing e-materials is often less labor-intensive than print materials, because statistics can be kept and reported automatically. You can develop a decent understanding of overall use and use patterns of e-resources by depending on vendor- and publisher-provided statistics. Many libraries are still taking the time and effort to collect their own statistics. This may involve the creation of complex reporting tools, but is often enlightening. For one thing, there is no standardization among the database vendors with regards to the basic statistical measures, including number of users, number of 'uses' of a product, and so on. Libraries that keep their own statistics can compare products across vendors with more confidence than if they rely on the vendors' data.

## Balance access options

As is mentioned above, many resources have overlapping coverage with competitors. It is up to the library to evaluate the best resources to purchase, taking into account such access issues as print vs. electronic, number of users, dates of coverage, format of records, etc. Conveniently offering both paper and electronic access in the library for the short term is one solution your library might stick with, as long as you have the room and the money. Other issues to consider include the impact on printing and copying services, storage and space concerns, staffing for e-resource troubleshooting vs. reshelving bound materials, your budget, and the needs of your patrons for distance-enabled materials.

## *Creativity*

You must be creative in how you offer access and guidance to your electronic resources. Librarians no longer hold all the keys to the doors of information. Prepare for creative responses by constantly reevaluating how users are using electronic materials. Practice creativity by being willing to try all new manners of activities to support evolving resources, and by learning from your mistakes as you experiment.

# Conclusion

Regardless of how technology transforms libraries and librarianship, it is important to remember that you are first and foremost a public servant. Without your patrons, customers, clients, users or whatever you choose to call them, there would be no library. It's easy to think you have a monopoly on information, but that is certainly not the case. Your patrons have lots of options to choose from, including the Internet and bookstores. Survey after survey show that many people turn to Google, or their friends, or Amazon.com before they ever think of turning to a librarian.

Regardless of how much technology changes libraries, certain things will always remain true. Because you most likely learned these points in library school, we will not take much space in this book to discuss them. Always keep the following points on public service in the back of your mind:

- Patrons have choices for their information needs.
- Taking time to answer questions is not an interruption, it's your job.

- Take ownership of your patrons' requests and needs.
- Never embarrass or match wits with your patrons.
- A patron's opinion of your entire library can be based on a single experience.
- Reward good customer service in your library.
- Have a basic proficiency in every core public service procedure in your library.

## Note

1. Internal Investigative Committee, Johns Hopkins University. Report of internal investigation into the death of a volunteer research subject [web document]. Baltimore, MD: Johns Hopkins University and Johns Hopkins Health System [rev. 16 July 2002; cited 15 October 2001].

## Further reading

Arant, Wendi and Mosley, Pixey Anne (2000) *Library Outreach, Partnerships, and Distance Education: Reference Librarians at the Gateway*. New York: Haworth Information Press.

Blake, Barbara Radke and Stein, Barbara L. (1992) *Creating Newsletters, Brochures, and Pamphlets: A How-to-do-it Manual*. New York: Neal-Schuman Publishers.

Cassell, Kay Ann (1999) *Developing Reference Collections and Services in an Electronic Age: A How-to-do-it Manual for Librarians*. New York: Neal-Schuman Publishers.

Garnsey, Beth A. and Powell, Ronald R. (2000) 'Electronic mail reference services in the public library,' *Reference and User Services Quarterly*, 39, 3: 245–54.

Gray, Edward and Langley, Anne (2002) 'Public services and electronic resources: perspectives from the science and engineering libraries at Duke University,' *Issues in Science and Technology Librarianship* (Summer); available online at: *http://www.istl.org/02-summer/article2.html*.

Katz, William (2000) *New Technologies and Reference Services*. New York: Haworth Information Press.

Kimmel, Stacey E. and Heise, Jennifer (2003) *Virtual Reference Services: Issues and Trends*. Binghamton, NY: Haworth Information Press.

Lankes, R. David and Collins, John Williams (2000) *Digital Reference Service in the New Millennium: Planning, Management, Evaluation*. New York: Neal-Shuman Publishers.

Lankes, R. David (2003) *Implementing Digital Reference Services: Setting Standards and Making It Real*. New York: Neal-Shuman Publishers.

Lubans, John (2001) '"To save the time of the user": customer service at the millennium,' *Library Administration and Management*, 15, 3: 179–82.

Walters, Suzanne (1992) *Marketing: A How-to-do-it Manual for Librarians*. New York: Neal-Schuman Publishers.

Whiting, Peter (2002) 'New frontiers in reference service: electronic serials transforming public service,' *Serials Librarian*, 42, 3–4: 211–16.

# 8

# Networking

You can make more friends in two months by becoming interested in other people than you can in two years by trying to get other people interested in you.

Dale Carnegie

The stereotypical politician is always making new contacts. He or she is constantly out shaking hands, kissing babies, and trying to develop a network of 'friends' who will support a bid for election. Or support a bill he or she is advocating, or support whatever the issue *du jour* might be. An extremely outgoing nature hardly resembles the stereotypical librarian, who sits in the library with all those tomes and is happy shushing people all day long.

We hope you know by now that the stereotype has long been false. In fact, being a professional librarian requires many more political skills than most people think. No matter where you are in your organization, if you want to climb to the top of this profession, you have to have the assistance of a network of friends. In this case, 'friends' are not necessarily people who like you and socialize with you on a Friday evening. 'Friends' in the professional context are the colleagues, clients, and associates who will recommend you for projects, promotions, and placements or who will help you in other ways in your career. Without friends, you lack the support needed to move up in your library or elsewhere. And finally, much of the work we do transcends the boundaries of departments. With the contacts you make networking, you will have an easier time gaining the support of people outside your department.

## Where and when should I be networking?

Motivation will almost always beat mere talent.

Norman R. Augustine

The simple answer to this question is 'everywhere and all the time.' Every person you meet is a potential contact in the future. This particularly holds true for your core library users, coworkers, staff, and student assistants, but it is also applicable to your family and friends, your neighbors, people you know from volunteer or social events, fellow members of your professional society, and total strangers on the bus. *Anyone* could be helpful to you at some point in the future – and you might be helpful to him or her.

Your network will need continuous maintenance, just like a fishing net. Imagine having a college friend call you out of the blue and ask for a major favor. You might feel piqued by having been ignored all those years, only to be turned to in a pinch. Your professional friends are likely to react the same way. In addition, some people may develop into closer contacts than others – these are the people who you can turn to for more help and guidance than others. Recognizing what kind of friend each person can and could be is an extremely valuable skill.

There are four major areas where you can build a network of friends. These areas can be described using a foursquare diagram that is commonly used in marketing to describe target groups, as shown in Figure 8.1.

**Figure 8.1** The librarian's friends foursquare

| | | Locational scale | | |
|---|---|---|---|---|
| | | Local | | Global |
| Library expertise | High | YOUR LIBRARY | | YOUR PROFESSIONAL SOCIETY |
| | | | YOUR INSTITUTION | |
| | Low | YOUR LOCAL COMMUNITY | | |

In Figure 8.1 the locational scale of the community (considered in terms of 'physical distance from me') runs along the x-axis while the degree of library expertise (or 'familiarity with what I do') runs along the y-axis.

The four major groups of people whom you are likely to encounter on a regular basis, and thus with whom you can network, are mapped onto the diagram. First are the people in your library. Your coworkers are both very close to you (they may be literally within arm's length) and have a high degree (one hopes) of familiarity with what you do. Second are the people in your professional society or association. Even the 'national' societies are becoming more and more global in their membership and their reach. You may see these people less than once a year. However, they are most likely librarians, and thus high on the library expertise axis.

Networking with other librarians, whether they are in your library or in your society, is a basic requirement of a successful career. It is the second two groups that may seem like less likely candidates for networking but who, in fact, can be better contacts. Faculty, staff, and administrators at your institution make excellent friends, but they may require the most effort to get to know. This is because they have neither a high degree of familiarity with libraries (in general) nor are they particularly close to you (physically or socially). Members of your local community (including civic, religious, and social groups to which you belong) are close to you in location, but may have only the barest understanding of what you do. Clearly these categorizations are generalizations and do not apply to every member of these groups – some of your contacts will belong to more than one, or to none in particular – but in general they will hold. Each requires a different approach to networking.

## Your library

Building a network of friends and supporters at work is one of the most important activities in your career. The reputation you build, and the connections you make among your immediate colleagues, translates directly into the opportunities you are given for advancement. These opportunities can be in the form of committee assignments, offers to work on prestigious projects and publications, or recommendations for promotion and tenure.

The first step in networking at your library is to go out and meet people. An easy way to do this is to attend library-sponsored events such as seminars, lectures, brown-bag lunches, and so on. Different departments in a large library often sponsor these events with the stated purpose of sharing information about a project, getting feedback on an idea, or for general education. If you have something to contribute, speak up. Introduce yourself to the people sitting next to you. After the event, introduce yourself to the person who organized it, and comment on the quality of the experience (if there was any).

Another important step is to familiarize yourself with the work of your colleagues – and for them to get to know your work. Volunteering for interdepartmental teams and committees is a great way to find out what is going on elsewhere in the library, as well as a good way to get to know people with whom you don't usually work. If you are not qualified to be on a team but are interested in the team's work, offer to be 'staff' to the team or committee. This involves such duties as taking minutes, securing meeting space, and processing materials. While this sounds like a dreadfully dull job, it can gain you a great reputation among team leaders who will come to appreciate your willingness to help. Search committees are also beneficial groups to volunteer for – you will not only meet people already employed by the library but also make the acquaintance of new candidates.

Finally, remember that you are not just a librarian but also a person. Your coworkers are people, too. It is critical for long-term success in any organization that you are not just a worker, but also a human being. It can be hard to break into the social circles of a library, but remember that your coworkers want to like you personally. They are probably curious about your non-work life, as you are of theirs. Do not shy away from social events at the library – they are both good for you and (often) lots of fun. Tag along with the lunch group. See if you can join (or start!) a book group or other after-hours social event. Attend the annual picnic or holiday party – with your significant other, if you have one. You will discover that being open to socializing with your colleagues strengthens your work bonds, in addition to building your community of social friends.

## Your professional society

There are a surprising number and variety of national and international professional societies and associations. Being an active member in at least one of these groups will be crucial for your professional advancement (discussed in Chapter 9 entitled 'Moving up'), not only because of the network of friends you can build on both national and global levels.

When you sign up for an association, you are usually given a choice of special interest groups (SIG) to which you can belong for free or for a small additional fee. Choose your SIG based on your professional interests. You will start getting information from your association, your chapter, and your group about membership and officers, upcoming meetings and conferences, and publication opportunities along with other announcements.

As with networking on the local library level, the crux of networking on the global level is the willingness to put yourself forward through volunteering for additional duties and through introducing yourself to other members. The easiest way to meet other people in your profession is to go to conferences and other meetings. Introduce yourself to the people who sit next to you in seminars or elsewhere in the hotel (you can usually tell they are with your conference by their name badge). Talk to presenters after their sessions. Go to poster sessions and talk to the presenters there. Seek out authors of papers you read (and remember) in school and complement them. Of all these techniques, the last is most likely to garner you a good reaction – people love to know that they have been read! They will be so excited to talk to someone who appreciated their research that they will ask all kinds of questions about what you do, and may even introduce you to other people they know at the conference. Give your business card to every person you meet – you'll probably get theirs in return. After the conference, use those cards to follow up people you found particularly interesting and with whom you'd like to keep in touch.

While at the conference, make sure you attend the planning or organizational meeting for your chapter and/or group. These are often sparsely attended, so you can get to know the leadership pretty quickly. Volunteer to help organize a panel session or other event for the next conference, or to co-organize one with a more 'seasoned' member. If you are feeling brave, offer to be an officer or an officer-in-training.

Many associations are now trying new ways of recruiting and retaining new members. Take advantage of these. Mentorship programs seem particularly popular right now. In these programs an experienced member is paired with a new member who has similar interests. You can also ask someone from your chapter or group to be your mentor on a less formal basis. Your mentor can then be a resource for your questions – from 'who's that?' to 'what should I go to next?' to more broad questions about where you should publish, what other positions are available, and what kind of research might be interesting.

Finally, go to all of the social events. Most conferences are replete with receptions, lunches, and banquets as well as with unstructured and informal gatherings at the hotel bar or restaurant. Remember: you are a person, not just a librarian. Some well-known and highly regarded professionals go to conferences solely for the social events, and skip the technical panels and seminars altogether. While your institution may disapprove of such behavior (particularly if you're being paid to attend the conference), such people definitely know a lot of people and have a lot of fun! Besides, experience has proven that incredible ideas can come out of informal conversations with colleagues in non-work situations.

## Your institution

Just as at your library, people at your institution want to think highly of you and see you as more than just a librarian.

Scaling up the networking activities suggested for your library will be effective for networking at the institutional level. For instance, you can volunteer to be a member of (or staff to) a university committee. You can attend university seminars and other special events. Institutions often have social events for their faculty. Keep an eye on calendars published in campus and division newsletters for notice of events that are open to the public and members of the institutional community.

Unlike your coworkers, people you meet at the institutional level have an inherently different relationship to you as a librarian. The people at your institution are probably both your peers and your clients. Many academic librarians are forced to function in a state of 'faculty limbo' where they are given some of the responsibilities of faculty, but not always all of the rights and perks. This may mean that some faculty will be tempted to treat you as a paraprofessional *unless* you take steps to raise your professional stature with them. However, faculty who discover exactly what you are capable of, including how you can help them with their teaching, research, and/or service goals, are usually more than happy to involve you in exciting projects at the institutional level. Clearly, serving on an institutional committee or co-teaching a university course greatly improves your professional capital.

## Your local community

At first blush it may not seem that making friends outside your professional sphere will help you much in your career. However, the people you know in 'real' life may intersect with your 'work' life in unforeseeable ways, such as if you move to a new institution or if they have positions in your institution of which you are currently unaware. They may know people at your institution who are decision leaders and – who knows? – your name could come up. Making friends socially is beyond the scope of this book, but the following tips could help you keep your professional needs in mind after hours.

- Talk about what you do. Your friends and acquaintances from your neighborhood, your place of worship, your child's school, or your volunteer groups may have no clue that you are a librarian. Talk about what being a librarian means, and what you do not just for your institution but also for the community. One of the authors has inspired at least three of her acquaintances to enter the profession (including one of the other authors)!

- Find out what your friends and acquaintances do. You may be surprised at the number of people you already know who work at your institution. Offer your professional services if appropriate.

- Volunteer your skills to your friends and groups as their librarian, historian, archivist, data manager, webmaster, etc. Be a volunteer consultant or committee member on a civic project.

- Always shine. Doing an excellent job as a volunteer can turn into excellent opportunities at your workplace, simply because someone familiar with your extracurricular activities recommends you for a work activity.

# What if I make enemies?

*Always behave like a duck – keep calm and unruffled on the surface but paddle like the devil underneath.*

Jacob Braude

Much as you might wish otherwise, not everyone you meet will like you. Stressing over it will probably only make matters worse. You may have conflicts with other people because of differences of opinion, conflicting personalities, or competition for promotions or positions. The world of academic librarianship is relatively small, so it would behoove you to keep your enemies list short. How do you do that?

- Try to defuse small issues before they explode into uncontrollable situations.

- Be aware of other people when you are making criticisms of their work or trying to move up in the organization. In particular, avoid stepping on toes with regard to pet projects, staff supervision, etc.

- Always give credit to the people who helped you on a project, including the person who gave you the idea. This needs to be done no matter how you feel about the person. It is the work that counts.

The best attitude toward people that you just don't get along with (or who, for some unknown reason, don't get along with *you*) is to leave them alone. If you do have to interact with the other person, there are some tips and strategies you can use to make the situation better:

- *Play nice.* When a person expects you to act in a negative manner, the best way to resolve the situation is to be positive from the start. Not only will the other person usually revise her opinion of you, it also puts you in a better light when evaluated by a third party.

- *Don't reciprocate.* This strategy means that you continue to play nice even if the other person has attacked you first. Continue to be rational even while the other person goes nuts. Try to imagine that the person has good intentions and respond in kind.

- *See past the person to their point.* Most people color what they hear by how they feel about the person speaking. However, even your worst enemy has good ideas at least once in a while (probably). Try to catch and highlight the good ideas rather than dismissing everything out of hand.

- *Compromise.* Finding the middle ground between two opposing ideas can be extremely difficult. People who are able to do this in the midst of tension are highly prized in most organizations for their people skills.

Sometimes you may end up with a situation of seemingly irreconcilable differences with another coworker. Sitting down to talk may help. Many institutions offer peer mediation services for situations like these. You might want to confer with a supervisor about ways to rearrange your duties so that you are taken out of direct conflict with the other person. It is always better to find a way to resolve the conflict by diplomatic means than to declare war on the other person. This is not only because you could sabotage your own career by appearing to be a problem employee, but also because you could do serious damage to the functionality of your library department.

## Conclusion

Whether we like it or not, where you are is often a factor of who you know, not what you know. We are suggesting that you take that piece of information and use it to your own and your library's advantage. Why fight a losing battle? Besides, you could get invited to a lot more parties through your networking activities.

## Further reading

One of the problems with suggesting further reading in the area of networking as a business concept is that most of the resources out there are aimed at sales and marketing professionals. Such texts talk about increasing your sales volume and commissions through aggressive networking. You may be uninterested in this kind of attitude toward your colleagues and clients. As a result, you may find more targeted information in a library management textbook. Listed below are some books specifically about networking in the business sphere.

Baker, Wayne E. (2000) *Achieving Success Through Social Capital: Tapping the Hidden Resources in Your Personal and Business Networks*. San Francisco: Jossey-Bass.

Berry, Jacky (2002) 'Managing your career,' *Library and Information Update*, 1, 2: 48–9.

Brinkman, Rick and Kirschner, Rick (1994) *Dealing With People You Can't Stand: How to Bring Out the Best in People at Their Worst*. New York: McGraw-Hill.

Burley-Allen, Madelyn (1995) *Listening: The Forgotten Skill*. New York: John Wiley & Sons.

Carnegie, Dale (1990) *How to Win Friends and Influence People*. New York: Pocket Books.

Catalyst (1999) *Creating Women's Networks: A How-to Guide for Women and Companies*. San Francisco: Jossey-Bass.

Catt, Hilton and Scudamore, Patricia (2000) *30 Minutes to Improve your Networking Skills*. London: Kogan Page.

Fisher, Donna, Vilas, Sandy and Hermance, Marilyn (2000) *Power Networking: 59 Secrets for Personal and Professional Success*, 2nd edn. Austin, TX: Bard Press.

Harris, Carol (2000) *Networking for Success: The NLP Approach to a Key Business and Social Skill*. Dublin: Oak Tree Press.

Kramer, Marc (1998) *Power Networking: How to Use the Contacts You Don't Even Know You Have to Succeed in the Job You Want*. Lincolnwood, IL: VGM Career Horizons.

Jette, Karen (1997) 'Conflict resolution,' in Joan Giesecke (ed.), *Practical Help for New Supervisors*. Chicago: American Library Association.

Solomon, Muriel (1990) *Working With Difficult People*. Englewood Cliffs, NJ: Prentice Hall.

Zaleznik, A. (1970) 'Power and politics in organizational life,' *Harvard Business Review*, May/June: 46–70.

Zand, Dale E. (1981) *Information, Organization and Power*. New York: McGraw-Hill.

# 9

# Moving up

Progress begins with the belief that what is necessary is possible.

Norman Cousins

Many academic librarians are evaluated for promotion and tenure decisions according to similar criteria to their faculty colleagues. These criteria are based on accomplishment and promise in three areas of scholarship: teaching, research, and service. One major difference for librarians, however, is that ahead of success in any of these other areas, the librarian must excel in her job. Ultimately, you have to learn how to create a balance between handling the demands of your job and the time it takes to publish or be a committee chair.

If you are presently at an institution where librarians do not have to go through promotion and tenure, that doesn't mean you never will be. Often in this profession, moving up involves moving out. It is a pretty safe bet that one day you will work at a 'tenure shop.' Therefore, if you already have some articles or committee work under your belt, so much the better. And finally, sharing your ideas and work can be extremely rewarding.

To get you started thinking positively about fulfilling the criteria, consider that in your case, 'teaching' can include most aspects of your job, since often your work responsibility probably involves some aspect of support to the academic programs of your institution. 'Service,' in the academic context, generally includes the work you do with scholarly and civic societies. Professional involvement in at least one scholarly society is a vital part of the service package for most academics. The most difficult aspect of scholarly advancement for many librarians to meet is 'research.' For the purposes of promotion and tenure, your research activities are demonstrated by your publications and presentations. This chapter will focus on the service and research aspects of 'moving up,' with some time spent, in conclusion, discussing the role of your résumé or curriculum vitae (CV) in your professional career.

# Getting involved in a professional society

> Action springs not from thought, but from a readiness for responsibility.
>
> Dietrich Bonhoeffer

It can be tempting to join every society that you are interested in. However, that can be very expensive and probably won't get you a very good return. A better option is to pick one or possibly two professional societies and to build your contacts and involvement there.

## Selecting a society to join

Which society, then? The options may seem endless. You could join one of the many library-specific societies, such as the American Library Association or the (UK) Library

Association. These groups tend to be especially large, extremely generalized, but very powerful. Getting involved on a national level may take time, but you will be very well-known and respected by a lot of people as a result. Another option is to join one of the smaller subject or library-type organizations, such as the (US) Association of College and Research Libraries and the American Society for Information Science and Technology. These groups still have international standing, but are more focused in their interests. Many non-library professional organizations have special interest groups for informatics. For example, chemistry librarians might join the Chemical Information Division of the American Chemical Society.

Once you have selected a few contenders for possible membership, investigate their major issues and interests by reading the associations' journals or magazines, exploring their websites, and leafing through their conference proceedings. Ask your colleagues about their involvement and experience with particular associations. If you are planning to get involved in a society, it is a good idea to attend at least one conference first. That way you will get to know the group dynamics – and you can assess your level of comfort with the group. This will dictate your long-term willingness to work with them.

## Getting involved in the society

Most societies are desperate for new people to get involved in their work. Getting involved is not hard. The tips in Chapter 8 on networking are equally as valid for getting started in a society as for meeting people at a conference.

## *Staying involved and moving up in the society*

The hard part about being involved in a society is staying involved. This can be particularly difficult if there are geographical and time challenges. You may see the members of your society just once a year and, most likely, they will not work at the same institution as you. However, after you have first joined and gotten involved in one or two projects, in spite of the challenges, you may feel ready to move on to new projects. Here are some tips for continuing involvement in professional associations:

- *Continue to be eager*. People will start asking you to join projects and committees, but not always the ones you want to be part of, or when you want to be part of them. Just as when you are starting off, you have to control your destiny by choosing whether to put yourself forward.

- *Be visible*. If you skip the annual meeting a couple of times people will assume you aren't an active member anymore. When you come back you'll essentially have to start over.

- *Recognize your limits and learn to say no*. Burnout is often a big problem in any organization that depends on volunteers – largely because volunteers aren't willing or able to turn down new opportunities. As librarians we are stereotypically nice people, and we want to make everyone happy. Don't worry about it – whoever asked you will probably just go and bug someone else if you decline.

- *Chart out a path and follow it – most of the time*. When you first join an association you may decide that you want to chair a certain committee or win a certain award.

Plan out how you'll do that, and stick to your plan. Recognize that you aren't likely to be elected to a national position immediately, but that you can take steps to build the recognition to make that dream possible. At the same time, if something really interesting pops up, try it – it may lead to a whole new life for you!

# Breaking into the world of research and publishing

> It is not because things are difficult that we do not dare; it is because we do not dare that they are difficult.
>
> Seneca

## What can I publish?

The short answer is: you can publish just about anything. Did you write a thesis or major paper for your degree? This is an excellent candidate for publication. Did you write a literature review, case study, or other term paper for a favorite class? Another good candidate. Many library journals publish pathfinders, 'webliographies,' or resource guides to subject literature. You can also get started as a book reviewer for one of the many journals and websites out there – publishers will usually send you the book for free (which you can then keep, sell, or donate to your library). Once people find out that you enjoy writing you will probably be asked to help with articles or even books. Other ideas for publication include conference reports, newsletter articles, lesson plans, instructional handouts and pamphlets, letters to the editor, etc. Remember: not everything must be peer-reviewed, particularly in the beginning. Your first push is to get your name recognized by being in print somewhere.

Many librarians write articles in a 'how we did this project' vein. Because you are writing about how you and/or your library solved a particular problem, you don't have to go out of your way to do research on top of your job. Also, many librarians begin their project planning by scouring the literature to see how others tackled the same problem. It is a good way to share creative solutions with the rest of the profession.

If you are thinking of tackling a research article, the hardest question to answer is: 'What can I research?' The answer will depend largely on what you do and in what you are interested. Most institutions will welcome research into the information needs and habits of their faculty, staff, and/or students. Collection use studies are relatively easy to set up and are very useful for cash- and space-strapped libraries. The same goes with studies of distance education and the library, the use of online resources, information retrieval studies involving the catalog or databases, and so on. Before you get started you may need to fulfill some administrative requirements, so make sure you check out the section on 'administrative hoopla' below.

## Where can I publish?

Again, the short answer is: almost everywhere. This is not to say that publishing in some underground rag will get you as much recognition as a peer-reviewed journal. You do want to select the places you publish carefully. Consider what audience the journal has. In general, you want to publish where your colleagues will see the article. This includes small subject or function-based journals, regional and national society magazines, and the large peer-reviewed journals. A good place to start is writing for online, subject-oriented journals. For example, all three of the authors have materials published in *Issues in Science and Technology Librarianship*, which is an online publication of the Science and Technology Section of the Association of College and Research Libraries. With the proliferation of new journals in librarianship, you may also have an easier time breaking into the world of publishing via a new journal than an established one. Finally, often publishers or editors will send out requests for articles or books. Don't be afraid to respond. That is precisely how we came to be writing this book.

Sending a manuscript to a journal for consideration is a nerve-wracking experience. You have no idea who will be reading and commenting on your paper. You're probably afraid that it will get rejected out of hand and sent back to you with negative comments about your intelligence. In reality, you will hear back from the editor in about six weeks to six months after sending off the paper (much less if the journal is entirely online). Rarely are papers rejected out-of-hand, but few papers are accepted 'as is.' Typically, you will get your paper back with suggestions for ways to strengthen it. You can increase your chances of your paper not returning to you if you employ the services of a good copyeditor. One of the authors always has her papers copyedited and has never had anything sent back for review.

Another way to avoid some of this heartache is to contact the editor or publisher in advance. Send her your idea for your paper, with an abstract if available. The editor will let you know whether she thinks your paper is appropriate for the journal, and may even make some comments about other publications they think you should consider using in your piece (our advice: pay attention to these!). Getting the go-ahead from the editor does not mean that your paper will be accepted, but it does indicate that you have a good chance.

## Alternatives to publishing

Preparing a manuscript for publication involves a lot of time and effort, much of it after you've finished your research and analyzed your results. A popular alternative is to present your research (or other wisdom) at scholarly conferences. In general, you can discuss your research based on a paper that you have contributed, you can be on a panel of experts, or your can present a poster. In the former case, your paper will be published in the proceedings; in the latter cases you will usually contribute an abstract and possibly your PowerPoint slides. Other alternatives include presenting at local meetings and lunches, teaching seminars, or writing for a website. On occasion, a publisher may approach you to turn your conference talk into a paper. It then becomes an 'invited' paper on your CV.

## The administrative hoopla

Before you embark on a research project you need to consider several administrative issues. It is generally considered unwise to push forward without completing the necessary steps for approval on each of these steps. The steps may vary even across departments in a library, so it is best to confer with your supervisor first.

- *Do I have time to do this research?* You may be one of the lucky few who can take a sabbatical or other time off from your regular duties to do library-related research. If you're not, you need to determine whether you can really spare the time to focus on research. You may need to work outside of your regular office hours to complete the research, analysis, and follow-up work. How will your supervisor and colleagues feel about you taking time off during work for this project? Make sure you discuss time issues with your supervisor before starting.

- *Do I have funding to do this research?* A lot of library research can be done using the computer on your desk, and does not require any additional (overt) outlay of funds. However, you might be producing surveys, mailing materials, or using staff time other than your own. There may be intellectual property issues associated with the use of institutional funds and materials (including staff), depending on how your institution's copyright policy is written. In your case, you need to determine whether your library will support your research or if you need to find external funding – such as a grant – to finance the project.

- *Does this research involve human study participants?* In the United States academic institutions are required by the federal government to review every study involving human subjects. Some institutional review boards require faculty and research staff to complete training before submitting research proposals. The board will review your proposal and approve or deny it, based on criteria designed to protect the safety (physical and emotional) of human study participants. Since this process can take a long time it is wise to start early.

- *Do I have permission to do this research?* This may be the crux of your research preparations. Make sure that your supervisor and the library's administration are aware of and have approved your research before you begin.

## Managing your intellectual property

A few weeks after your first paper is accepted for publication, you may receive a copyright transfer agreement in the mail. Your publisher may inform you that, as a condition of publication, you must sign and send back this contract immediately. Be careful! Read the contract first – preferably with someone who is familiar with contract law and intellectual property issues. You may be surprised to discover that you are signing away the ownership of your article (your work!) to the publisher, and that you will no longer have some rights with regard to the contents. These can include the right to publish the article later in a compilation, the right to reuse a table or image in another paper, and the right to photocopy the article for use in your classroom or to give to your colleagues. A huge debate is underway between publishers and academics about copyright issues – be savvy and get involved in it!

# Bringing it all together: creating and maintaining your CV

Your CV is a critical aspect of your application for a job, promotion or award, and should be as strong and as up to date as possible. Some libraries will ask you for an updated CV every year as part of your evaluation. Even if you don't have one yet, now is the time to start. Keep in mind the following basic 'rules' for writing your CV:

- *Revise, revise, revise!* Update your CV on a regular basis – every time you do *anything,* update your résumé. Do you have a new job function? Have you taught a new class? Learned a new database? Joined a new committee? Add it! This way the document will always be current and you'll never have to scramble at the last minute when applying for a job.

- *Target it to the reader.* Sending the same CV to several potential employers only works if you are applying for the same job at each place. Modifying your CV each time to highlight your particular interest in that position not only makes you look good, it also helps you figure out what your interest in that particular position is!

- *Get lots of feedback.* Make sure you ask other people to read your CV before you send it off. They will probably find typos, odd grammatical constructions, and superfluous or missing information. Take their comments and put them to good use!

- *No typos!* There is nothing more embarrassing in applying for a new position than to discover that you misspelled your job title. Trust us, even if you don't catch it, the person seeing the document for the first time will, and it *will* affect their opinion of you.

Your curriculum vitae (CV), résumé, website, published biography, and any other available information about you creates a picture of you by which people will judge your qualities and abilities. The CV is a powerful tool that can be used in a variety of different situations. At its most basic, your CV is the factual outline of your professional life. Potential employers will use it as a guide to see if your qualifications match the responsibilities and expectations of their open position. If your CV is public it can also be used by people who wish to know more about you (e.g. people looking to nominate you for awards, speeches, select societies, etc.). Your CV can also be useful as an outline for people looking for speaker introduction fodder, or for your department to keep on file as an indication of the expertise available in the library.

## Types of CVs

Why a CV and not a résumé? It is common, in academic circles, to use a fully fleshed-out CV when job hunting rather than the traditionally short (one page, most likely) résumé. This is largely because academic libraries are looking for candidates who show promise in all three faculty competency areas – teaching, research, and service. The longer CV, with categories for such things as your publications, demonstrates this much more clearly than the short résumé could.

There are three major types of CV:

- *The chronological CV.* This type calls for a list of your professional history in date-completed order. This type can be good for new librarians or for people who have just switched careers, as it will highlight your education over your employment history.

- *The functional CV.* If you chose this type, you would group items by their functions – so you could group your education, experience, and skills according to their relevance to instruction, collection management, management, etc.

- *The combination CV.* This is the type most often used and combines elements from both the chronological and functional CVs. By grouping information into sections according to type (see some suggestions, below) and listing them chronologically within the section you get a very logical progression of information.

The next decision to make, after choosing a type for your CV, is in what format you wish to create it – online or in print. Many professionals create versions in both formats. Make them stylistically similar, but otherwise you can be creative. For instance, experiment with hyperlinking your online publications and teaching portfolio into your CV, or play with borders and layouts on your print CV. The online CV has advantages in terms of interactivity and flexibility with length, but the print CV is more portable, easier to file, and easier for you to control its presentation (because you don't have to worry about differences in browser functionalities).

## *Structure of the CV*

The information you include in your CV will vary according to a variety of factors, including the immediate purpose for the document, the types of activities you have done, and the amount of space you wish to use. Some basic information, however, should appear on every CV. Your name and contact information are required. The bare facts about your employment and educational history must be on every document (as applicable). From here, however, your options broaden out considerably.

Optional sections of the CV include:

- objective – a statement of your immediate and/or long-term career goals;
- skills – foreign and computer languages, computer and database competencies, etc.;
- continuing education activity – courses, workshops, seminars, etc. you've taken;
- instruction – courses, workshops, seminars, etc. you've led or taught;
- publications – peer-reviewed articles as well as other items including book reviews, pathfinders/resource guides, major newsletter articles, and major internal library documents;
- presentations – talks you have given not only at conferences, but also to student groups, brown-bag lunch groups, etc.;

- professional activity – dates of membership for any societies and associations as well as committee or group memberships, volunteer activities, etc. related to the societies;

- committee memberships – groups that you have been a part of in your various positions, with the dates of membership and any special role you might have played (e.g. staff, chair);

- volunteer activity – only if your work outside your institution is applicable to your career and the purpose of the CV (*applicable* is the key word);

- personal information – hobbies, interests, and other random cool stuff about you.

Remember that you will be evaluated according to the teaching, research, and service standards of your institution. As the factual representation of you on paper, your CV should reflect your accomplishments in each of these areas. It is strongly recommended that the full CV include, as applicable and appropriate, sections for teaching (instructional 'presentations' as well as major print and electronic materials you may have produced), research (you can conflate 'publications' and research-based 'presentations'), and service (you can conflate 'professional activity,' 'committee memberships,' and 'volunteer activity').

Since many institutions like to see personal and professional growth in their faculty, information about your skills and continuing education activities may also be appropriate. The objective may help focus a scattered CV, and can be particularly helpful if you are seeking a career change. Finally, many interviewers want to know something human about each candidate they consider – you should not be surprised to be asked 'what do you do in your free time?' – so including something interesting in a hobbies or personal information section may make you stand out.

## References

Most people include a statement such as 'References: available on request' to keep the identity of their references confidential. However, a list of three to four people willing and qualified to give you a positive review should always be at hand. Make sure you keep up with them – not only with their lives, but also with their changes in job title and contact information. These people can make or break your chances of success in getting a promotion or a new job. Interviewers will ask them in-depth questions about your skills and their perception of your ability to perform well in the new position.

Unless there are serious conflicts, your immediate supervisor will be one of your references. A potential employer may contact your boss even if she is not an 'official' reference. When you are first starting as an academic librarian, you may have to ask one or more of your professors from school to be references. This is fine, but eventually you will need to include people who are more familiar with your professional than your student work. Other good candidates may include faculty who are familiar with your work, colleagues, members of your academic society with whom you have worked closely, and former supervisors.

The No. 1 requirement of a reference: make sure he or she will give you a good review!

# Conclusion

It is never too late to begin building your portfolio, if only to fulfill your obligation to the profession by sharing with your colleagues all of that terrific knowledge you have acquired. You owe it back to the profession that, we hope, has given a lot to you. Share the wealth!

# Further reading

## *Getting involved*

The resources listed in Chapter 8 on networking will be helpful to you on this subject as well.

## *Research and publishing*

Your bookshelf is not complete without a variety of style guides, to which you should refer early and often. Guides to the MLA, APA, and Chicago Online styles will be the most helpful.

Alley, Brian and Cargill, Jennifer (1986) *Librarian in Search of a Publisher: How to Get Published*. Phoenix, AZ: Oryx Press.

Black, Dolores et al. (1998) *500 Tips for Getting Published: A Guide for Educators, Researchers, and Professionals.* London: Kogan Page.

Booth, Wayne C., Colomb, Gregory G. and Williams, Joseph M. (2003) *The Craft of Research.* Chicago: University of Chicago Press.

Crawford, Walt (2003) *First Have Something to Say: Writing for the Library Profession.* Chicago: American Library Association.

Duranceau, Ellen Finnie (1993) 'Publishing opportunities: getting into print or getting involved,' *Serials Librarian,* 23, 3/4: 253–6.

Kester, Norman G. (1997) 'How to get published,' *Feliciter,* 43 (May): 8.

Kitta, Donna (1986) 'How to publish in ALA periodicals,' *Ohio Media Spectrum,* 38 (Summer): 50–7.

Nofsinger, Mary M. (1991) 'Librarians and book publication: overcoming barriers,' *Reference Librarian,* 33: 67–76.

Penaskovic, Richard (1985) 'Facing up to the publication gun,' *Scholarly Publishing,* 16 (January): 136–40.

Pitts, Judy M. (1985) 'Scoring points with professional publication,' *Arkansas Libraries,* 42 (March): 26–30.

*Publish Your Article Outside the Library Field: A Bibliographic Guide to Non Library and Information Science Journals with Articles on Libraries, Librarians, or Library Service.* Chicago: American Library Association, Office for Human Resource Development and Recruitment for the Library Instruction Round Table, 2000.

Schroeder, Carol F. and Roberson, Gloria G. (1995) *Guide to Publishing Opportunities for Librarians*. New York: Haworth Press.

Sellen, Betty-Carol (1985) *Librarian/Author: A Practical Guide on How to Get Published*. New York: Neal-Schuman Publishers.

Thomson, Ashley (1987) 'Librarian as author: the perils of publishing,' *Canadian Librarian Journal*, 44 (August): 93–6.

## The curriculum vitae

Beatty, Richard H. (2002) *175 High-Impact Résumés*. New York: J. Wiley & Sons.

Heiberger, Mary Morris and Vick, Julia Miller (1996) *The Academic Job Search Handbook*. Philadelphia: University of Pennsylvania Press.

Newlen, Robert R. (1998) *Writing Résumés That Work: A How-to-do-it Manual for Librarians*. New York: Neal-Schuman Publishers.

Parker, Yana (1993) *Résumé Pro: The Professional's Guide*. Berkeley, CA: Ten Speed Press.

Ream, Richard (2000) 'Rules for electronic résumés,' *Information Today*, 17, 8: 24–5.

# 10

# Leadership

We have placed the section below concerning the role of the supervisor at the beginning of the leadership chapter for a reason. The best supervisor has the ability to lead people – not boss them around. The last section of the chapter, the role of the leader, covers the basic tenets of leadership with examples, where appropriate, for the academic librarian.

## The supervisor's role

> Treat people as if they were what they ought to be, and you help them to become what they are capable of being.
>
> Johann Wolfgang von Goethe

### Definition of the role

We think that the best way to supervise people is to be very clear with yourself about what your role is as a supervisor. And that role can be summed up very neatly:

A supervisor is responsible for making sure that her employees have everything they need to do their job well.

So what does 'everything they need' include? Good question. This is where it can get tricky. We have provided you with a list below of the basics, but you will need to remember whenever you encounter a supervising problem to ask yourself the question, 'What do I need to do to make sure this employee has what they need to do their job well?'

So what are any employee's needs?

1.  a clear understanding of what the duties of their job are;

2.  complete training for all of their duties;

3.  someone to communicate on their behalf with superiors and other departments;

4.  all supplies and equipment necessary to do their job;

5.  a trusting relationship with you, their supervisor;

6.  the opportunity to make mistakes and learn from them;

7.  development and learning opportunities;

8.  the opportunity to make their jobs fun;

9.  to be treated like an adult, no matter what their job entails;

10. within reason, to be helped to find work that is meaningful and that they are able to do well.

## Employee assessment

As the supervisor, one of your main responsibilities is to assess your employee's abilities to do the job they are in. Ultimately, if they are not capable of carrying out the duties of the job, especially after being given the appropriate training, feedback, supplies, and support, then you have to enlist their help in understanding that this may not be the position for them. No one likes to be in a job that they are not able to do, or do well. And if they cannot work for you, your final responsibility to them is to help them understand that it isn't the right job for them. Then you must offer to help them look for other employment that they are better able to do.

The assessment is your opportunity to share with your employee your thoughts on how well they are doing their job. You can praise efforts well done and share with the employee the areas where you think they need to improve. The assessment meeting can be a place where you can learn from them how well they think they are doing. If you have built a trusting relationship with your employees, this sharing of information will go very smoothly.

> This is a test. It is only a test. Had it been an actual job, you would have received raises, promotions, and other signs of appreciation.
>
> Anonymous

The following tips for writing employee assessments are based on guidelines from the book *Effective Phrases for Performance Appraisals* (Neal, 2002: 201–5):

- Rate objectively. You can improve your objectivity by avoiding these approaches:
  - *The halo effect.* When an evaluator rates a person good or bad in all areas based on experience or knowledge of the employee in only one dimension.

- *Leniency tendency*. Evaluating all employees as outstanding rather than assessing them on their individual performance.

- *Strictness tendency*. The opposite of the leniency tendency: evaluating all employees at the low end of the scale and a tendency to be highly critical.

- *Average tendency*. A tendency to evaluate all employees as average regardless of differences in performance.

■ Use significant documentation and factual examples.

- Have your employees submit monthly reports to you on their activities. Create a template for them to use which lists the major areas of their jobs. When it comes time to write their evaluations you will have all of the factual evidence on hand to use instead of relying on your, most likely, overloaded memory.

- Create documentation throughout the year on your employee's activities. An easy way to keep this documentation organized is to create a file for each employee that includes their monthly reports as well as any statements you have written (and dated) about their performance throughout the year. You can also place into their files examples of some of their best (or worst) work.

- When writing evaluations you will want to make sure you are relating an employee's performance to their job description. Use the documentation and the monthly reports to describe specific examples of their performance.

- Examples need to be specific and objective. You must refrain from subjectivity and generalizing.

- When you are able, use quantitative facts that can be expressed in numerical terms such as 'Increased journal check-in load by 35 per cent' rather than 'Sped up journal check-in.'

■ Plan well for the appraisal or evaluation meeting. This meeting is one of the most important meetings you will have with your employees. You want to make sure that it is effective and, if at all possible, non-threatening.

  - Select a quiet, comfortable and appropriate location.

  - Avoid interruptions. Make sure someone else is available to answer the phone and handle visitors.

  - Allow plenty of time for discussion.

  - Put the person at ease by smiling at them and remaining calm.

  - Conduct the interview in a positive manner.

  - Review each rating by category, if appropriate.

  - Keep the interview performance-oriented. Remember to focus on the work, not the person.

  - Encourage the employee to talk.

  - Listen actively and carefully.

  - Avoid being defensive. If you are not prepared to answer a question, write it down and tell the employee you will look into it. Then do so, and get back to them later.

  - Focus on patterns of behavior, not on isolated incidents.

  - Respond as positively as possible to objections, problems, and disagreements.

  - Concentrate on the facts.

- Be honest, especially about your own performance. If something was your own doing, say so.

- Be a coach not a judge. Remind them that mistakes are fine as long as they learn from them.

- Emphasize positive reinforcement.

- Work together on developing positive action plans.

- Bring the interview to a close with positive and supportive words.

■ Emphasize future development. The most effective appraisals and evaluations stay focused on the future. When you can attain the goals of the organization and maximize employee growth, you will have true success. You can increase your own and your employee's potential when you:

- create strategies together for strengthening areas where the employee needs to improve;

- develop a plan based on mutual goals (yours and the employee's), which will prepare the employee for greater responsibility;

- set up scheduled follow-up meetings to give the employee feedback along the way;

- always use positive reinforcement to motivate your employees.

■ Emphasize the positive. As you will discover when you read the leadership tenets listed at the end of this chapter, when you focus on the positive you keep people from putting up their defenses. If you can keep them from becoming defensive, they will be more likely, and possibly better able, to make positive change.

Only positive consequences encourage good future performances.

Kenneth H. Blanchard

## Problem employees

In the middle of difficulty lies opportunity.

Albert Einstein

Now that we have laid out the supervisor's role and how to assess your employees, you are probably waiting to hear our words of wisdom on what to do about the problem employee. Not to oversimplify, but in our experience, most problem employees fall into two categories: those who have not had their needs met and those who are not in a job they are capable of doing.

For employees who have not had their needs met, your first step will be to figure out what their needs are. Do they need a more structured work environment? Or do they need less structure? Are they having difficulty coping with certain aspects of their job, or difficulty with people they come into contact with at work? Sometimes, fulfilling an employee's needs is not possible in the work environment and you may have to refer them to employee counseling or some other outside resource.

When people come to work they do not leave their personalities or personal lives at home. Once you acknowledge that you are managing the whole person and not just their work performance, the easier it is for you to respond to each employee's individual needs. Remember to find people's strengths and build on them. As supervisors, we are responsible for getting the right people to do the right things so that the work gets done. By building a relationship of trust, you will increase your chances of having your employees tell you what they need to get their jobs done. It all goes back to the importance of building trust.

Now to get back to the other type of problem employee: the one who is not capable of doing the job he or she is in. These are the employees with whom you must work closely. The best way to approach this type of employee is to take their side. Set up a meeting with them to go over very carefully all of the requirements of their position. With their input, create a training timeline that will ensure that they are given every opportunity, within reason, to learn all of the skills they need to perform their job well.

If, at the end of the training period, they cannot demonstrate proficiency in the required tasks, this is now the point when you have to help them take ownership of the problem. Tell them that you need someone in this position who can do all of the required activities well and that even though they worked very hard, their skills are not a good match with the requirements of the job. At this point it is helpful to list for the employee the skills they *do* have, describing for them what they do well, and finally you can offer to support their effort to find a position where they *can* excel.

## The real *problem employee*

In a case where the two approaches above do not work, your only real resource is your documentation. Almost every academic institution has policies and procedures laid out for how to handle problems with employees. Ask the personnel librarian for support, or contact the university human resource office for information on how to proceed. In the meantime, document all employee actions. Write up descriptions of employee actions and your response to them in a signed and dated document that you keep in the employee's file. Actions are easier to track when you use a performance log to track and record behaviors. You can also use this log as a guide when providing feedback to the employee. Elements of the log include:

- employee name;
- date documented;
- the event: what happened, when, where, who was involved; list specific behaviors; list specific outcomes;
- the expectations: what are the standards, the desired outcomes, the performance factor, the managerial factor;
- the impact: on you, others, the department, the organization;
- the action taken: what, who, how, by when.

Keeping a log will help you keep all of the information organized so that you are prepared to handle any difficulties that may arise from the actions of the problem employee. It will also help you to think clearly about the employee's performance because all of the information you need will be clear and organized.

## The role of the leader

> Management is doing things right; leadership is doing the right things.
>
> Peter Drucker

Firstly, there are so many good books on leadership. Our challenge is how to condense this vast amount of information into a usable guide for you. We will offer some tips on basic behaviors that will get you started, but the real challenge is the one that you will have to make for yourself. The roles and responsibilities of leaders are far more difficult to achieve than any skill we have talked about in the previous chapters because they often involve phenomenal personal commitment to change yourself. A few of the tips below make an appearance in the previous chapters. You can think of this final chapter as a summing up of the roles of the academic librarian. We all have to be leaders to help our academic libraries make a full transition into an electronic environment. So much will change before we get there that no person in the institution can sit idly by as if nothing has changed.

And secondly, a leader is someone who gets positive things done within their organization. Leadership is not about winning, or having your ideas carried out every time, or being in charge. Ultimately it is about working well within a group. Leadership can be found anywhere, at any moment, and can be practised by any member of the organization. It exists when people think beyond the realm of the self to the larger realm of the organization. Leadership is inspired by vision and belief, and is continued by personal reinforcement of the right kind of behavior.

One more quote:

> A sense of humor is part of the art of leadership, of getting along with people, of getting things done.
>
> Dwight D. Eisenhower

For many dedicated and, yes, even serious people, if work isn't fun, it isn't worth doing. If it isn't fun we get burned out. If we are burned out we don't produce good work and can harm ourselves and our organizations. So a secondary aspect of leadership is – how can we make work fun? When reading through the tips below, think of how you can insert humor into your own interpretation of them.

This chapter began with the basics of supervision, beyond those such as delegation and running meetings. However, you must always remember that leadership often starts at the supervisor level. So by keeping leadership ideas in mind when supervising, you will be able to stay focused on the goal – getting things done.

## Leadership – what is it?

Let's begin with the basic essence of leadership – leadership is any action which furthers progress toward the goal. Once you grasp this one definition, you will then have a litmus test for anything you do. If you are wondering why a project is stalled, or you can't get the support you need for a project, stop and ask yourself what are the things that are in the way of progress occurring. What leadership tip can you follow to get the project moving again?

Below is a list of basic tips on how to be a leader taken from our own study of the literature on leadership. Many of them focus on the attributes of leaders and are the most appropriate for an academic library setting. Some of them may at first seem out of place in a discussion on leadership.

But remember, if it furthers action, it is leadership. If it in any way stagnates or reverses progress – don't do it, because it isn't leadership. So, what can you do to become a leader? Try on a few of these hats and see what happens. Because there are so many, they are in alphabetical order.

## Accept and embrace ambiguity

The world is an ambiguous place. Nothing is set in stone or certain to happen. We often have to act without knowing all of the facts. Waiting until we do know all of the information is equal to inaction. And inaction will get you nowhere or even worse than nowhere. If you can let go of your desire for control, you will have freed yourself and will be able to confront constant ambiguity. You will not be frozen with indecision when something surprises you. You will expect the surprise and be able to handle it. You will be able to find out what you *can* do with the information you *do* have. After you accept that nothing will ever be truly complete or final, or perfect, then you can make progress.

> My basic principle is that you don't make decisions because they are easy; you don't make them because they are cheap; you don't make them because they're popular; you make them because they're right.'
>
> Theodore Hesburgh

## Be kind

More work will get done faster if requested in a kind manner. Give people water and sunshine and see how they blossom.

## Change yourself and you change how people respond to you

Perceptions are often true reflections of reality. Even if they aren't, on an individual level, what you perceive is what you know. Knowing this, and knowing that you cannot change anyone but yourself, and that if you don't like the way certain people are – change how *you* react to *them*. One of the authors calls this 'the good intentions rule' – assume that everyone has good intentions. Very few people can really know how others perceive them. So if you act as if others actually have good intentions, no matter how they are behaving towards you, and you respond to them as if that were true, then even if their intentions are bad, you will have a profound effect on them by your (surprisingly) positive response.

## Do your homework

By this we mean be prepared. Read reports before the meeting rather than during the discussion about what's in them. Come to meetings with a list of things you want to make sure will be covered. Do assignments on time. Pull your weight on big projects. When people at work know you are prepared for things and can be depended on to follow through, you will have won their respect. And with respect comes trust.

## Find your strengths and accept the strengths of others

One of the authors loves to be on committees with people who like to copyedit, because she hates copyediting. If others improve on her writing, she thinks it is terrific. What this person *does* like doing is banging out a first draft, so she often volunteers to write one. Then she sends it out to the group for them to change whatever they see fit. She trusts that with all these different eyes looking at it, the final version can only be that much better.

## Flexibility is vital

Be willing to change directions midstream. Don't get tied to finishing a project for the sake of finishing it. If the end project is not worthwhile, stop and change direction.

## Focus on the work not the person

And the converse is true. Don't take comments about your work, or the work of your group personally. Remember – assume good intentions and accept other's perspectives. So, when offering comments on work, talk about work – don't name or blame the people.

## Have a personal stress management technique and use it

Getting stressed does no one, least of all ourselves, any good. Find and learn some techniques that work for you when the going gets tough. One of the authors, when she is having a particularly horrid day, stops and tries to consider what the previous day or a day from the week before was really like. Was she angry? Sad? In a terrific mood? Most of the time she can't remember how she felt. Then once she realizes that she can't remember, she accepts that however strongly she feels about something right now, tomorrow it won't matter as much.

## Have a clear plan toward reasonable goals

If we don't know where we are going, how can we get there? Knowing what you are working toward is just the beginning. Without a process in place to guide you toward your goal, your actions will be haphazard at best. Don't be afraid to ask what the goals are in any work situation. From the one-on-one interactions to large library meetings, if you are at any time unsure of the goals, you can be sure others are too. Raise your hand and ask for help in understanding the final goals. It will help everyone clarify their own work.

> Goals are dreams with deadlines.
>
> Diana Scharf Hunt

## Influence is stronger than demands

If people like you, trust you, and value your opinion, they will fall over themselves to help you. Just by reading this book you are taking a powerful step toward being a positive force to reckon with in your library. Getting people excited about working on a project with you is a much more powerful motivator than getting your boss to ask their boss to tell them to help you on a project. Think about it.

## Learn positive negotiating techniques

Much of what you do at work will be easier if you know the basics of good negotiation. One of the books listed at the end of this chapter is quite probably the best book on basic negotiation, *Getting to Yes* by Fisher and Ury (1991). Get it. Read it.

## Lose your ego at work

We don't mean stop trying to be the best you can be. We mean think of your work as something in progress, not as an extension of your personality. This is especially pertinent if you are part of a group. If people disagree with something you have written, or an idea you have put out, it doesn't mean that they are attacking you personally. It simply means that they have a different way of thinking about things. The most productive thing you can do if someone disagrees with you is to ask them, in a nonconfrontational way, what is important to them? How would they propose the action gets carried out? Remember, the end product is the most important thing. If you are spending time quibbling over the tiny details, are you moving forward to the goal?

No one is perfect, no matter how hard they want to believe it, it will never be true. So, be humble. Accept that others will have ideas that you have not yet thought of nor ever will.

## Make connections

Constantly think about the broad picture or environment. When considering any decision, think about the effect it will have on the entire organization. And if you don't know what effect it will have, ask others how it will affect them. When making plans for a project, think about how it relates to other projects happening in the library or on campus. Who could be an ally or a consultant to your project? Who are the possible stakeholders?

## No whining

If you want to change something instead of complaining about it, offer solutions. People are much more willing to listen to a person with ideas rather than a naysayer. And we all know that complaining is seldom welcome and rarely listened to. If you don't have any ideas on how to change something, suggest that you are willing to work with others to find better solutions.

> Whining is not only graceless, but can be dangerous. It can alert a brute that a victim is in the neighborhood.
>
> Maya Angelou

## Optimism

Be open to new ideas, and new ways of doing things – even the untried and seemingly silly.

> Minds are like parachutes – they only function when open.
>
> Thomas Dewar

## Send angry e-mails to yourself instead of the person you are mad at

Then read it 24 hours later. If you still feel strongly, send it. Ninety-nine percent of the time you won't send it because you will realize that no reply is the best action to take. Always ask yourself – will replying further the action?

## Thank people for their work – it is one of the most powerful motivators

Take the time to verbally, or with a written note, thank people for their efforts. Even if their work has little to do with you, thank them. If you attend a meeting that someone did an exceptional job of organizing – send them a thank-you note. So seldom are people recognized for a job well done. We usually only hear if we are not doing well. And in the end nothing will inspire people more than a simple thank you.

> You have it easily in your power to increase the sum total of this world's happiness now. How? By giving a few words of sincere appreciation to someone who is lonely or discouraged. Perhaps you will forget tomorrow the kind words you say today, but the recipient may cherish them over a lifetime.
>
> Dale Carnegie

## There is no hierarchy

Every single person who works in the library is vital to its success. When one person fails, there is a snowball effect.

Respect the efforts of everyone at work from the people who clean your office to the director. Operate as if there is no hierarchy and everyone will want to support your efforts.

## Trust that you cannot know everyone's experience

If someone describes a situation that for them is entirely different than it is for you, don't argue or think that they must be wrong – trust them, especially if they are having difficulty with something and are asking for help. We cannot know what their experience is like because we are not them. The true leader will trust and offer help instead of arguing with someone. Instead of saying – 'well, it isn't like that for us,' ask them how you can help them.

## Turn your negative emotions into positive action

If you are angry and irritated about someone or something at work the best thing to do is to figure out how to react positively. Reacting negatively will only worsen the situation. If someone is undermining your reputation or your project, don't respond in a negative fashion. Don't let it affect your work. If you have serious concerns about your working relationship with someone at work, share them in a non-blaming way with your boss or a colleague, and ask for their advice on how best to handle the situation.

## Use criticism, constructive or not, as an opportunity for increasing your self-awareness

See 'lose your ego' above. Criticism can be a powerful gift. It is so difficult to see ourselves how others see us. Armed with their feedback, use it to chart out a plan to be better.

> Criticism is prejudice made plausible.
>
> H.L. Mencken

# Conclusion

> Experience is not what happens to you; it's what you do with what happens to you.
>
> Aldous Huxley

> Success is peace of mind which is a direct result of self-satisfaction in knowing you did your best to become the best you are capable of becoming.
>
> John R. Wooden

Now that we have filled your head with practical advice, what are you going to do with it? The authors hope that you are now better prepared to make your work environment one that is much more productive and definitely more fun to be in. We hope that this book is just one of many that you read in your journey to excellence. The lists of further reading are just the tip of the iceberg. Don't hesitate to look beyond the profession for resources to help you work 'better' and 'smarter.' Don't despair if you find bad management or organizational politics getting in the way of your best work. Do some research. Figure out what you can do to change things from within, or even from the bottom up. We hope we have given you some practical tools that you will find useful. If not, we hope that you will write a book that tells us how to do it better. If you do write that book, let us know. We will want to read it.

## Further reading

Blanchard, Kenneth H. and Johnson, Spencer (1982) *The One Minute Manager*. New York: William Morrow.

Brudvig, Glenn L. (1992) 'Managing the sea change in science and technology libraries,' in Cynthia A. Steinke (ed.), *Sci-Tech Libraries of the Future*. New York: Haworth Press.

DuPree, Max (1992) *Leadership Jazz*. New York: Currency Doubleday.

Fisher, Roger and Sharp, Alan (1998) *Getting It Done: How to Lead When You Are Not in Charge*. New York: Harper Perennial.

Fisher, Roger and Ury, William (1991) *Getting to Yes: Negotiating Agreement Without Giving In*, 2nd edn. Boston: Houghton Mifflin.

Frank, Donald G. (1998) 'Leadership in science-engineering libraries: considerations and realities for the future,' in Cynthia A. Steinke (ed.), *Sci-Tech Libraries of the Future*. New York: Haworth Press.

Goleman, Daniel (1998) *Working With Emotional Intelligence*. New York: Bantam Books.

Hirsh, Sandra Krebs (1996) *Work It Out: Clues for Solving People Problems at Work*. Palo Alto, CA: Davies-Black.

Kouzes, James M. and Posner, Barry Z. (1995) *The Leadership Challenge. How to Keep Getting Extraordinary Things Done in Organizations.* San Francisco: Jossey-Bass.

Lockett, Barbara (1992) 'Scientific and technical librarians: leaders of the 21st century,' in Cynthia A. Steinke (ed.), *Sci-Tech Libraries of the Future.* New York: Haworth Press.

McClain, Gary, and Romaine, Deborah S. (2001) *The Everything Managing People Book.* Avon, MA: Adams Media Corporation.

Max, Douglas and Bacal, Robert (2003) *Perfect Phrases for Performance Reviews: Hundreds of Ready-to-Use Phrases that Describe Your Employees' Performance (from 'Unacceptable' to 'Outstanding').* New York: McGraw-Hill.

Mintzberg, Henry (1992) 'Managers and leaders: are they different?', *Harvard Business Review*, March–April: 126–35.

Neal, James E., Jr (2002) *Effective Phrases for Performance Appraisals: A Guide to Successful Evaluations*, 9th edn. Perrysburgh, OH: Neal Publications.

Pickering, Peg (2000) *How to Manage Conflict: Turn All Conflicts into Win-Win Outcomes*, 3rd edn. Franklin Lakes, NJ: Career Press.

# Index